T0207422

Lecture Notes of the Institute for Computer Sciences, Social Informatics and Telecommunications Engineering 551

The LNICST series publishes ICST's conferences, symposia and workshops.
LNICST reports state-of-the-art results in areas related to the scope of the Institute.
The type of material published includes

- Proceedings (published in time for the respective event)
- Other edited monographs (such as project reports or invited volumes)

LNICST topics span the following areas:

- General Computer Science
- E-Economy
- E-Medicine
- Knowledge Management
- Multimedia
- Operations, Management and Policy
- Social Informatics
- Systems

Teresa Pereira · John Impagliazzo ·
Henrique Santos · Juan Chen
Editors

Internet of Everything

Second EAI International Conference, IoECon 2023
Guimarães, Portugal, September 28–29, 2023
Proceedings

 Springer

Editors
Teresa Pereira 🆔
University of Minho
Guimarães, Portugal

Henrique Santos 🆔
University of Minho
Guimarães, Portugal

John Impagliazzo 🆔
Hofstra University
Hempstead, NY, USA

Juan Chen 🆔
National University of Defense Technology
Changsha, China

ISSN 1867-8211   ISSN 1867-822X (electronic)
Lecture Notes of the Institute for Computer Sciences, Social Informatics
and Telecommunications Engineering
ISBN 978-3-031-51571-2   ISBN 978-3-031-51572-9 (eBook)
https://doi.org/10.1007/978-3-031-51572-9

This Springer imprint is published by the registered company Springer Nature Switzerland AG
The registered company address is: Gewerbestrasse 11, 6330 Cham, Switzerland

Paper in this product is recyclable.

Preface

It is a pleasure to introduce the proceedings of the second edition of the European Alliance for Innovation (EAI) Internet of Everything Conference (IoECon 2023). The Internet of Everything (IoE) has brought together researchers from around the world who are leveraging and developing community research on a concept that intelligently connects not only devices but also people, processes, data, and things. This conference focused on a complete ecosystem that interconnects everything, such as people-to-people, people-to-machines, and machines-to-machines, emphasizing technological effects on people and organizational processes, as well as a meaningful discussion about the competencies required on an Internet of Everything curricular course to respond to the accelerated technological evolution.

The technical program of IoECon 2023 consisted of eleven accepted papers, covering most of the conference's topics, which were presented over two days at the main conference track. Aside from the high-quality technical paper presentations, the technical program also featured one keynote speech by Xiuzhen Cheng, Professor of Computer Science at Shandong University, China, addressing the Blockchain-enabled High-confidence Internet of Things, and one roundtable discussion organized by Natalie Kiesler from Leibniz-Institute für Bildungsforschung, Germany, with the invited participation of Teresa Pereira and Henrique Santos, both Professors from the Information Systems Department of the University of Minho, Portugal, John Impagliazzo, Professor Emeritus of Hofstra University in the USA, and Juan Chen from National University of Defense Technology, China.

The Information Systems Department of the Engineering School of the University of Minho supported the conference organization. Coordination with the Steering Committee chairs, Henrique Santos, John Impagliazzo, and Juan Chen, was essential for the conference's success. We sincerely appreciate their constant support and guidance. Working with such an excellent Organizing Committee team who worked hard to organize and support the conference was also a great pleasure. We are also grateful to the Conference Managers, Kristina Havlickova and Viliam Farkas, for their support and to all the authors who submitted their papers to the IoECon 2023 conference.

We strongly believe that the IoECon conference provides an excellent forum for all researchers, policymakers, developers, and practitioners to discuss all relevant science and technology aspects of IoE. We also expect to meet you again at the IoECon 2024 conference, helping us make it an even more relevant event for consolidating the IoE ecosystem and developing the IoE community.

Teresa Pereira
Juan Chen
Natalie Kiesler
Henrique Santos
John Impagliazzo

Organization

Steering Committee

Juan Chen	National University of Defense Technology, China
John Impagliazzo	Hofstra University, USA
Teresa Pereira	University of Minho, Portugal
Henrique Santos	University of Minho, Portugal

Organizing Committee

General Chair

Teresa Pereira	University of Minho, Portugal

TPC Chair and Co-chair

Natalie Kiesler	DIPF Leibniz Institute for Research and Information in Education, Germany
Henrique Santos	University of Minho, Portugal

Publications Chairs

António Amaral	Polytechnic Institute of Porto, Portugal
Isabel Mendes	University of Aveiro, Portugal

Panels Chairs

Henrique Santos	University of Minho, Portugal
Eliana Stravrou	Open University of Cyprus, Cyprus

Local Chair

Teresa Pereira	University of Minho, Portugal

Technical Program Committee

Hala Alrumaih	Imam Mohammad Ibn Saud Islamic Univ., Saudi Arabia
António Amaral	Polytechnic Institute of Porto, Portugal
Luís Barreto	Polytechnic Institute of Viana do Castelo, Portugal
Casey Bennett	Hanyang University, South Korea
Olga Bogoyavlenskaya	Petrozavodsk State University, Russia
Héctor Cancela	Universidad de la República, Uruguay
Juan Chen	National University of Defense Technology, China
Paolo Ciancarini	University of Bologna, Italy
Alison Clear	Eastern Institute of Technology, New Zealand
Ernesto Cuadros-Vargas	Latin American Center for Computing Studies (CLEI), Peru
Mats Daniels	Uppsala University, Sweden
Judith Gal-Ezer	Open University, Israel
Andrii Galkin	O.M. Beketov National University of Urban Economy, Ukraine
Ulrike Hugl	University of Innsbruck, Austria
John Impagliazzo	Hofstra University, USA
Raúl Junqueira	DST Group, Portugal
Natalie Kiesler	DIPF Leibniz Institute for Research and Information in Education, Germany
Nuno Lopes	Polytechnic Institute of Cávado e do Ave, Portugal
João Paulo Magalhães	Polytechnic Institute of Porto, Portugal
Linda Marshall	University of Pretoria, South Africa
João Matos	DST Group, Portugal
Andrew McGettrick	Strathclyde University, UK
Isabel Mendes	University of Aveiro, Portugal
Henrique Santos	University of Minho, Portugal
Safiya Al Sharji	University of Technology and Applied Sciences, Oman
Eliana Stavrou	Open University of Cyprus, Cyprus
Gerrit van der Veer	Vrije Universiteit, The Netherlands
Abhijat Vichare	ACM India, India

Contents

Machine-to-Machine (M2M)

Using the Internet of Everything
for High-Performance Computing

Zihan Zhang[1], Juan Chen[1(✉)], Sitan Liu[1], and John Impagliazzo[2] (iD)

[1] College of Computer Science and Technology, National University of Defense Technology,
Changsha 410073, Hunan, China
{zihanzhang,juanchen,liusitan20316}@nudt.edu.cn
[2] Hofstra University, Hempstead, NY, USA
john.impagliazzo@hofstra.edu

Abstract. In today's world, the demand for big data and computing power has made High-Performance Computing (HPC) popular among various fields. Super-computing as one of the representatives of HPC applications, the combination with the Internet of Everything (IoE) in its usage cycle cannot be ignored. For HPC, the Internet is the fundamental prerequisite for interconnecting multiple computers. The IoE enables more devices to be connected and extends how HPCs can be used. The Internet of Everything will affect the applications between HPC and various fields more deeply by connecting people, data, and machines. This paper provides an overview of the history of the Internet of Everything and HPC. It also shows the interaction issues between humans and HPC for the Internet of Everything. The Internet of Everything is widely used and has been shown to impact the HPC field profoundly. There is great potential for developing the Internet of Every-thing and HPC in the coming years and combining the two to drive multi-domain development.

Keywords: Internet of Everything · HPC · supercomputer

1 Introduction

The emergence of the Internet has brought people closer to each other, and the emergence of the Internet of Things (IoT) has made it possible to connect all things together and realize the interconnection of all things. The Internet of Everything has penetrated every aspect of people's lives. The Internet of Everything is a vast network that combines people, processes, data, and things, interacting and exchanging real-time data between components, an extension and expansion of the Internet of Things [1]. In terms of supercomputing, people (users and managers), data, and supercomputing form a system that can interact in two ways. Raw data is more valuable and influential due to the interconnection of everything. Supercomputers with many computer nodes cannot be more effective if they cannot communicate with each other, between computer nodes, between supercomputers and supercomputers, or between supercomputers and users, and only perform stand-alone operations.

© ICST Institute for Computer Sciences, Social Informatics and Telecommunications Engineering 2024
Published by Springer Nature Switzerland AG 2024. All Rights Reserved
T. Pereira et al. (Eds.): IOECON 2023, LNICST 551, pp. 3–10, 2024.
https://doi.org/10.1007/978-3-031-51572-9_1

From accessing only sporadic devices to the Internet of everything, the intelligent application of network technology brings great convenience. HPC can serve as the intersection of data collection and utilization and provide more intelligent services for human beings according to the needs of users [2].

This paper provides a brief overview of the inextricable relationship between the Internet of Everything and HPC. The article introduces the background of the development of the Internet of Everything and HPC, outlines the impact of the Internet of Everything on HPC, and lists the relationship between existing supercomputing and the Internet of Everything. It also outlines the importance of the Internet of Everything in HPC and an outlook on future development. Finally, the article discusses the combination of IoT and HPC to drive growth in multiple fields.

2 Background of IoE

The foundation of the Internet of Everything is the Internet. The Internet originated in the 1960s when the U.S. Department of Defense commissioned the development of ARPANET to research the Internet [3]. The earliest network formed was the ARPANET, with only four nodes, based on a report by Larry Roberts. As the number of computing nodes increased, the NCP protocol initially used needed to be revised to support the accurate location of information between different kinds of computers. The TCP/IP protocol proposed by Wynton Cerf and Robert Kahn solved this problem and significantly advanced the development of the Internet. In the 1980s, to share computer and network resources, the National Science Foundation established the NSFNET wide area network to make the Internet available to the entire community. Academic groups, corporate R&D groups, and individuals could share the computing power of NSF's giant computers and communicate with each other.

The Internet of Things (IoT) [4] is the third wave of information industry development after the development of the Internet. IoT is a more extensive, complex network formed by connecting Internet-connected devices that can sense and share data and securely interact with each other based on Internet protocols. IoT extends the user side to communicate at the item level. The world-famous "Troy Coffee Pot" is a portable camera installed next to the coffee pot to transmit coffee status information to a personal computer so that people can check it at any time [5].

The Internet of Everything is seen as the next phase of the Internet of Things and will be the future of society. The Internet of Everything (IoE) combines people, processes, data, and things that make network connections more relevant and valuable [1]. The Internet of Everything is driving the market for new applications in the communications industry, profoundly affecting how people travel, work, educate, and more.

3 Background of HPC

High-performance computing (HPC) [6] is widely used to solve performance-intensive and complex problems in defense, science, and finance by aggregating computing power using multiple computers and storage devices, with the advantage of high speed and low cost. HPC can run locally, in the cloud, or a hybrid mode [7].

Table 1. The Development of HPC

Machine	Year	Phase
Cray-1 (LANL)	1976	Vector
Cray X-MP (Digital Productions)	1982	Vector
Cray Y-MP (NASA Ames)	1988	Vector
Thinking Machines CM-5 (LLNL)	1993	MPP/SMP
Hitachi SR2201 & CP-PACS (Tokyo and Tsukuba)	1996	MPP/SMP
Intel ASCI Red (SNL-1 teraflop)	1997	MPP/SMP
IBM ASCI White (LLNL)	2000	MPP/SMP
NEC Earth Simulator (JAMSTEC)	2002	Clusters
IBM Blue Gene/L (LLNL)	2004	Clusters
IBM Roadrunner (LANL-1 pataflop)	2008	Clusters
Cray Titan (ORNL)	2012	Clusters
NUDT Tianhe-2A (NCSS Guangzhou)	2013	Clusters
Sunway TaihuLight (NCSS Wuxi)	2016	Clusters
IBM Summit HPE (ORNL)	2018	Clusters
HPE Acquires Cray	2019	Clusters
Fujitsu Fugaku (Japan RIKEN)	2020	Clusters

The development of HPC can be divided into four phases: vector machines, SMP, MPP, and clusters [8]. The first generation of high-performance computers was the vector computer named the Cray machine which appeared in the 1970s [9]. Vector machines add vector flow components to computers to improve computer performance, such as CDC series and CRAY series. Due to the high cost of vector machines, SMP (Symmetric Multiprocessor) was born, an architecture where a relatively small number of processors are installed inside the computer. All processors share memory and data bus, so SMP is high-performance, cost-effective, and compatible with standard hardware and software devices of the time. The MPP (massively parallel processing) [10] architecture was proposed to overcome the poor scalability of SMP. MPP consists of multiple independent microprocessors and uses a dedicated high-speed Internet to collaborate on tasks through software. The fourth stage of HPC development is clustering. Cluster system integrates various IT technologies in one, and at the same time, has low cost and high scalability, which is now the mainstream of HPC development. There are many areas where cluster architecture is applied, such as cloud computing and supercomputing [6]. Representative computers of different stages are listed in Table 1.

Unlike standard computing systems that primarily use serial computing to solve problems, HPC performs massively parallel computing and has high-performance computing components that guarantee the computing power of the cluster.

Due to the increasing demand for processing large amounts of data and the decreasing cost of usage, HPC technology has gained wide popularity in various fields. Generally, users can enjoy HPC services using locally deployed infrastructure or cloud resources. In addition, we can use HPC for weather forecasting, climate modeling, energy research, and intelligence processing, involving the processing of large amounts of data and millions of changes in the associated data points [11].

4 Impact of the IoE on HPC

In the late 1980s, the emergence of high-performance computing pushed supercomputing from a small number of professionals to a broader range of users. At the same time, the pursuit of metrics changed from a requirement for supercomputing arithmetic power alone to a comprehensive plan of high performance.

Jupyter [12] serves as an entry point for users to use HPC. Jupiter is a rich user interface that facilitates user interaction with supercomputers. It can be the entry point for users on HPC. Jupyter serves as an interface to the HPC hub and can be used as a platform for innovation. Users can systematically extend access to more shared nodes on Cori. A modular extension framework for JupyterLub that addresses some of the challenges users face on their laptops. For example, some new integrations are generated: file system navigation system, batch queues, and shared template notebooks.

Jupyter implements a new model of interactive supercomputing integration that allows code, analysis, and data to be brought together under a single visual interface with seamless access to powerful hardware resources. Jupiter developers work at the intersection of project and HPC centers and have built networks of contacts to collaborate and learn from each other.

5 Impact of the IoE on Supercomputers

A supercomputer is a high-performance computing cluster in which a dedicated or high-speed IB network connects numerous computers. Supercomputers include state-of-the-art hardware and software systems, testing tools, and algorithms for solving complex computations. Supercomputers seek high computational speed, and their benchmarks are focused on testing floating-point speed.

Typically, IoE is understood as the bridge that connects spaces such as people's homes with commercial and mobile environments (see Fig. 1) [1]. During the study of supercomputing, as shown in Fig. 2, the Internet of Everything connects users, data, and things into a whole, which includes person-to-person (P2P), machine-to-machine (M2M), and person-to-machine (P2M) systems. The person-to-person (P2P) system includes four interactions: administrator-to-administrator (A2A), administrator-to-user (A2U), user-to-administrator (U2A), and user-to-user (U2U). The machine-to-machine (M2M) system contains two parts: different supercomputing centers cooperating and the HPC interconnection network collecting data from each computer node. The human-to-machine (P2M) system results from the different requirements of experts in different application areas, and the supercomputing centers provide powerful computing power to domain-oriented experts. While advancing science, it also drives the development of more powerful supercomputers.

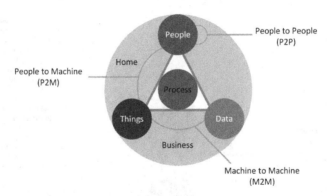

Fig. 1. Internet of Everything (See Fig. 1 in [1])

6 The Future of the IoE and HPC

The development of HPC is at a crossroads [6]. Semiconductor technology limitations and market forces are affecting the growth of HPC innovation. Denard scaling and the end of Moore's Law have continued to drive up the cost of manufacturing HPC systems. Cloud services companies should invest more deeply in the HPC market, and HPC with a leading edge is rarely seen as a business opportunity. Cutting-edge HPC systems need to rethink and re-build hardware and software configurations, revolutionize historical approaches, and face new challenges in the market [13].

The rapid development of the Internet of Everything puts new demands on HPC, and the centralized computing and processing model can no longer meet the needs of multiple business models. A new technology has emerged - the small distributed edge-based HPC, which provides end users with cloud computing resources and storage capabilities [14]. The dramatic growth in connectivity and increased data traffic of IoT devices has increased the need for edge-enabled HPC with low latency. Compared to traditional HPC, edge-enabled HPC can reduce processing time, provide data processing and management services, and take up much less space.

Edge-enabled HPC and emerging IT technologies are combined and developed, and new business forms are born and come into people's lives. For example, Telematics, smart classrooms, and AR/VR technology [15–19]. The future HPC industry will see bipolar development: edge-based HPC that conducts latency-sensitive services at the edge and traditional HPC systems that require centralized storage, deep processing, and analysis of large amounts of data. Edge-enabled HPC is also the first entry point for a wide range of data sources, forming a vast network. In addition, HPC will also converge with big data to analyze big data and run simulations and other HPC loads through the same large-scale computer clusters, more powerfully advancing groundbreaking research and innovation.

Cloud computing, edge computing, and end devices can be used as an infrastructure for IoT to bring computing closer to the end devices. The rapid growth in the computational demand for HPC systems has led to edge-level and cloud-level tiers being considered together for energy optimization and scheduling. Li et al. [20] comprehensively quantify the carbon footprint of HPC systems, considering both the hardware

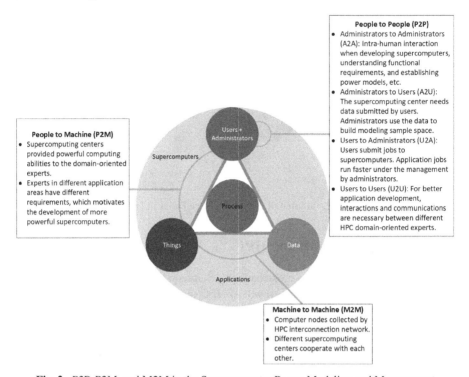

Fig. 2. P2P, P2M, and M2M in the Supercomputer Power Modeling and Management

production and system operation phases. Lin et al. [21] propose a multi-layer federation learning protocol called HybridFL that implements different aggregation strategies at the edge and cloud levels. Experiments demonstrate that HybridFL significantly speeds up the FL process and reduces the system energy consumption by reducing the length of short federation rounds and accelerating the convergence of the global model. Hou et al. [22] designed a hardware/software co-design solution AMG for multimodal artificial intelligence systems. AMG features a novel decoupled modal sensor structure and supports a new intelligent power management strategy that reduces the energy consumption of the modal sensors while ensuring system accuracy.

Artificial Intelligence and Edge Computing combine to solve the problems posed by the limits of Moore's Law. NVIDIA has created a performance-oriented Streaming Reactive Framework (SRF). The framework standardizes HPC streaming data pipelines to build modular and reusable pipelines for sensor data [23]. APS is a machine that generates photon beams to study materials, physics, and biological structures. Most of the inversion process can be avoided by using artificial intelligence when generating material images with nanoscale resolution via photonography, and deploying PtychoNN models trained in data centers on edge devices can increase image processing speed by more than 300 times.

7 Discussion

The combination of the Internet of Things and high-performance computing drives growth in multiple areas.

Within the traditional field of HPC, applications focus on more than just areas dominated by the solution of partial differential equations. Still, they are also expanding into new areas of development in conjunction with new technologies. HPC machines are not "general purpose" platforms, which poses several challenges for various applications in an HPC environment. Weßner et al. [24] have developed a framework, Geneva, for the parallel optimization of large-scale problems with a highly nonlinear quality surface. They created a new network component, MPI Consumer, that conforms to the standard paradigm of HPC programs. The powerful computing power of HPC contributes significantly to the simulation of physical systems. Galen et al. [25] provides a detailed quantitative analysis of representative simulations. He argues that to maximize the value of HPC computing power, emphasis should be placed on the deep synergistic development of hardware and software.

Based on edge computing, more and more devices have become mobile or non-mobile computing platforms. Along with the development of machine learning, sensors, and other technologies, IoT devices are equipped with intelligent and interconnected computing systems while maintaining their original functions. IoT devices have three main functions: sensing, communication, and computing. Telematics is to use the vehicle as an independent computing platform, sensing the environment through devices such as cameras and sensors, performing data analysis as well as computation of in-vehicle applications within the forum, and accomplishing the communication between vehicle and vehicle, and vehicle and cloud, which solves the problem of the transmission delay of the data in the large-scale Internet. Zhang et al. [26] proposed to build an open in-vehicle data analytics platform for automatic driving OpenVDAP, with an operating system that realizes the computation, communication, and security and privacy protection of the vehicle and provides optimal strategies based on real-time information of vehicle dynamic detection. Smart home pays more attention to the ubiquitous sensing ability of edge nodes, studies the fusion design of wireless sensing and wireless communication, and combines machine learning to build personalized models to ensure the privacy and security of user data. Huang et al. [27] explored the potential of smart homes using non-contact respiratory monitoring, pervasive sensing of devices through sound and electromagnetic signals, co-design of sensing and communication signals, and finally optimization of computation and communication overhead.

References

1. Kiesler, N., Impagliazzo, J.: Perspectives on the internet of everything. In: IoECon2022 (2022)
2. Higginbotham, S.: Network included - [Internet of Everything]. IEEE Spectr. **57**(11), 22–23 (2020). https://doi.org/10.1109/MSPEC.2020.9262153
3. Leiner, B., et al.: A brief history of the internet. Comput. Commun. Rev. **39**, 22–31 (2009). https://doi.org/10.1145/1629607.1629613
4. Khvoynitskaya, S.: The IoT history and future. Online (2019). https://www.itransition.com/blog/iot-history

5. https://bbs.huaweicloud.com/blogs/308804
6. Reed, D., Gannon, D., Dongarra, J.: HPC forecast: cloudy and uncertain. CACM **66**(2), 82–90 (2023)
7. Chen*, J., et al.: More bang for your buck: boosting performance with capped power consumption. Tsinghua Sci. Technol. **26**(3), 370–383 (2021). ISSN 1007-021. https://doi.org/10.26599/TST.2020.9010012
8. Wang, R., et al.: Brief introduction of TianHe exascale prototype system. Tsinghua Sci. Technol. **26**(3), 361–369 (2021). ISSN 1007–0214. https://doi.org/10.26599/TST.2020.9010009
9. https://www.cnblogs.com/laxcus/p/14666901.html
10. https://blog.csdn.net/ieee2007/article/details/5974472
11. Chen, J., Ghafoor, S., Impagliazzo, J.: Producing competent HPC graduates. Commun. ACM **65**(12), 56–65 (2022). https://doi.org/10.1145/3538878
12. Thomas, R., Cholla, S.: Interactive supercomputing with jupyter. Comput. Sci. Eng. **23**(2), 93–98 (2021)
13. Dong, Y., Chen*, J., Tang, Y., Wu, J., Wang, H., Zhou, E.: Lazy scheduling based disk energy optimization method. Tsinghua Sci. Technol. **25**(2), 203–216 (2020). https://doi.org/10.26599/TST.2018.9010140
14. Kong, X., Wu, Y., Wang, H., Xia, F.: Edge computing for internet of everything: a survey. IEEE Internet Things J. **9**(23), 23472–23485 (2022). https://doi.org/10.1109/JIOT.2022.3200431
15. Badia, R.M., Foster, I., Milojicic, D.: Future of HPC. IEEE Internet Comput. **27**(1), 5–6 (2023). https://doi.org/10.1109/MIC.2022.3228323
16. Bauer, M., Lee, W., Papadakis, M., Zalewski, M., Garland, M.: Supercomputing in python with legate. Comput. Sci. Eng. **23**(4), 73–79 (2021)
17. Kline, C.: Supercomputers on the internet: a case study. ACM SIGCOMM Comput. Commun. Rev. **17**(5), 27–33 (1987). https://doi.org/10.1145/55483.55487
18. Sato, M., Kodama, Y., Tsuji, M., Odajima, T.: Co-design and system for the supercomputer "Fugaku." IEEE Micro **42**(2), 26–34 (2021). https://doi.org/10.1109/MM.2021.3136882
19. Biryal'tsev, E.V., Galimov, M.R., Elizarov, A.M.: Workflow-based internet platform for mass supercomputing. Lobachevskii J. Math. **39**, 647–654 (2018). https://doi.org/10.1134/S1995080218050050
20. Li, B., Samsi, S., Gadepally, V., Tiwari, D.: Sustainable HPC: modeling, characterization, and implications of carbon footprint in modern HPC systems (2023). arXiv:2306.13177
21. Wu, W., He*, L., Lin, W., Mao, R.: Accelerating federated learning over reliability-agnostic clients in mobile edge computing systems. IEEE Trans. Parallel Distrib. Syst. **32**(7), 1539–1551 (2021)
22. Hou, X., et al.: Architecting efficient multi-modal AIoT systems. In: Proceedings the 50th International Symposium on Computer Architecture (ISCA) (2023)
23. https://developer.nvidia.com/zh-cn/blog/facing-the-edge-data-challenge-with-hpc-ai/
24. Weßner, J., Berlich, R., Schwarz, K., et al.: Parametric optimization on HPC clusters with Geneva. Comput. Softw. Big Sci. **7**, 4 (2023). https://doi.org/10.1007/s41781-023-00098-6
25. Shipman, G.M., et al.: The future of HPC in nuclear security. IEEE Internet Comput. **27**(1), 16–23 (2023)
26. Zhang, Q., et al.: Openvdap: an open vehicular data analytics platform for Cavs. In: 2017 IEEE 38th International Conference on IEEE Distributed Computing Systems (ICDCS) (2018)
27. Huang, Q., Li, Z., Xie, W., et al.: Edge computing in smart homes. Comput. Res. Dev. (9) (2020). https://doi.org/10.7544/issn1000-1239.2020.20200253

Using the Internet of Everything for Data Centers

Rongyu Deng[1], Juan Chen[1(✉)], Xinghua Cheng[1], and John Impagliazzo[2] (iD)

[1] College of Computer Science and Technology, National University of Defense Technology, Changsha 410073, Hunan, China
{dengrongyu21,juanchen,cxhchengxinghua}@nudt.edu.cn
[2] Hofstra University, Hempstead, NY, USA
john.impagliazzo@hofstra.edu

Abstract. With the new infrastructure in recent times, the data center is relevant to all lives. Whether an individual, a small company, or a large corporation interested in education, finance, telecommunications, retailers, or social networking services, data centers provide a convenient and efficient platform for storing and computing data. In other words, data centers connect users, administrators, servers, data and information, different machines, and devices. This expresses the concept of the Internet of Everything (IoE). In this paper, the authors analyze the profound connection between data centers and the Internet of Everything concept from three aspects: the historical development of data centers, the current development pattern, and the future development trend. Hence, the development of data centers is inseparable from the Internet of Everything concept, and many of the design ideas of data centers fit well with the Internet of Everything concept.

Keywords: Internet of Everything · data centers · people-to-people (P2P) · people-to-machine (P2M) · machine-to-machine (M2M)

1 Introduction

In today's rapidly evolving connected world, the Internet of Things (IoT) [1] is no longer a new word. Its significance is to connect independent physical devices to the internet or other devices, thus interconnecting machines and devices. But the Internet of Everything (IoE) as a recent concept is beyond this understanding because its connectivity is more comprehensive than devices and the internet. It has expanded to physical devices, people, processes, data, and other elements [2, 3], just like its name – 'everything'. In this context, almost everything is online and connected via the internet, while data transfers (almost) occur in real-time.

Moreover, due to content-based communication, artificial intelligence (AI) [4], and machine learning [5], every interaction helps IoE devices become "smarter" [1]. Therefore, IoE covers a broader range of areas, plays more roles, and is more adaptable to the rapid development of technology. The current widely used data centers can also be seen as a reflection of the concept of the Internet of Everything.

© ICST Institute for Computer Sciences, Social Informatics and Telecommunications Engineering 2024
Published by Springer Nature Switzerland AG 2024. All Rights Reserved
T. Pereira et al. (Eds.): IOECON 2023, LNICST 551, pp. 11–18, 2024.
https://doi.org/10.1007/978-3-031-51572-9_2

Data centers are the basic physical unit that carries data, a specific device network for global collaboration to deliver, accelerate, display, calculate, and store data information on the internet. Generally speaking, data centers are mainly composed of several parts: a computer room (building itself), power supply and distribution system, refrigeration system, network equipment, server equipment, storage equipment, etc. They could be applied in all aspects of production and life, essential to the digital transformation of various industries, and promote the rapid development of the digital economy [6]. There are three primary forms of data centers: physical data centers, IDC (internet data centers), and cloud computing data centers. In a 2021 report on digital infrastructure, real estate giant CBRE found that new data infrastructure in the U.S. broke ground and increased by 42% year-on-year, with data center service providers making several large land purchases this year to prepare for the next phase of development [7]. The result of data centers plays a crucial role in this era.

Data centers' primary function is to provide a space for companies like education, finance, telecommunications, retailers, and social networking services that process much information daily to carry all the data calculations. These generate and use data companies directly in data centers of virtual space and cloud computing resources pool to run their business. Therefore, they do not need to undertake new civil engineering room, cabinets, UBS, precision air conditioning, jumper, and so on room environment construction of the server, storage, network equipment procurement, and shelves, as well as the development of a business system, and deployment, availability reliability, and security operations [8]. This aligns with the concept of people in the Internet of Everything linking with machines, devices, and data through the internet [6]. In addition, from the perspective of the composition of data centers, many servers connect through the internet and constitute a large computer room environment for data storage and computing. It also reflects the close connection between the data and its equipment.

This paper aims to outline the historical development of data centers and the concept of the Internet of Everything, the operation mode of data centers in the present era, and the development trend of data centers in the future, and illustrate the inseparable relationship between data centers and the concept of the Internet of Everything. That is, data centers are a concrete embodiment of the Internet of Everything.

2 Background of Data Centers and IoE

Table 1 provides a brief history of data centers in the IoE context. With the introduction of the Electronic Numerical Integrator and Calculator (ENIAC), the first fully automatic electronic data computer in the 1940s, a new era of human computing was revolutionized, and the evolution of the "Data Centers" went with it began.

In the 1960s, the prototype of data centers began to emerge. Computer systems, storage systems, power equipment, and other related components had been discovered, but there needed to be a systematic connection between them; they were placed in the same space. The nascent data center was called a "Server Farm" to house computer systems, storage systems, electrical equipment, and other related components. At this time, the concept of interconnection was just beginning to emerge, as the first distributed control network, the Apha network, was first constructed in 1968 [9].

Table 1. History of data centers and IoE

Years	Machine	Stage meaning
1940s	Electronic Numerical Integrator and Calculator	A new era of computing
1960s	Server Farm	A prototype data center
1968	ARPANET	The first distributed control network
1990s	Client-server	The prototype of a traditional computer room
1990s	DC-IDC	The data center as Enfo eService
2005	IoT	Networked devices that sense and share data
2006	Cloud Data Centers	The rise of cloud computing

In the early 1990s, with the development of communications technology and the widespread use of computers, the micro-computing industry (servers) saw a boom, and the data centers concept began to develop. Connected network devices replaced the older generation of PCs, and the emergence of the client-server technology model [10], in particular, led to the creation of a separate room for servers, with simple equipment wiring, linking, and layering, using the term 'data centers' to name the space. At that time, the term 'data centers' became popular and was the earliest form of the traditional server room we have today. By the mid-1990s, the rise of the internet had a significant impact on the market. Internet connectivity has become a must for businesses to deploy IT services. Network providers and colocation providers were widely developed in creating hundreds of data centers, and most companies accepted data centers as a service model. At this point, the idea of relying on the internet for human-to-machine and machine-to-machine connectivity in IoE has begun manifesting itself. With the advent of mobile devices and wireless technology, fixed devices, which were difficult to move, have evolved into easily portable and mobile devices. The connection between man and device has also changed from one where people follow the device to one where the device follows people [2].

Since the beginning of the 21st century, the internet has seen explosive growth, driving the rapid development of data centers and showing a diverse trend. With the rise of global internet companies such as Google, Baidu, Tencent, and Sina, the PC boom required uninterrupted networks, promoting the rapid development of data centers, which became more professionally built and costly to maintain compared to before. It was not until 2005 that the data center's design, construction, and operation developed steadily. And it was in this year that China Telecom launched its highly industry-recognized server room design standard, namely: China Telecom - 2005 IDC Product Specification [11]. At the same time, the US telecom industry also promulgated the "TIA942 Standard" [6], which classifies server rooms into four levels, Tire1-Tire4. These two standards have played a normative and guiding role in developing data centers.

Furthermore, with the rise of cloud computing technology, cloud data centers are gradually coming into the limelight, integrating the computing, storage, and network layers into a single hardware device to achieve data centers management through a hyper-converged architecture, which has been called "hyper-converged architecture data centers." Furthermore, in 2005, the Internet of Things (IoT) concept was also introduced [12, 13]. Today, IoT refers to connected devices that can sense and share data, i.e., machine-to-machine connections (M2M) in the Internet of Everything concept [14].

3   Impact of IoE on Data Centers

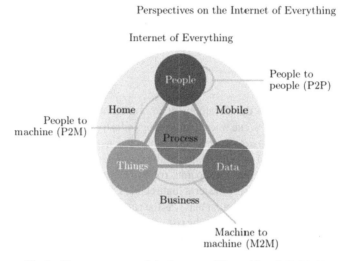

Fig. 1. The components of the Internet of Everything (IoE) [1, 2]

As shown in Fig. 1, IoE mainly comprises five components: personnel, machinery, equipment, data, and process, connected through the internet. Compared with the Internet of Things, which only emphasizes the connection between machines and devices (M2M), the Internet of Everything adds the relationship between people (P2P), the connection between people and machines and devices (P2M), and these ideas are correspondingly reflected in data centers [1].

For establishing the connection between people, machines, and equipment, the storage and calculation of data by the user or company with the help of data centers fall under the concept of P2M. The connection between data centers and users can be divided into three types according to the platform model the data center delivers to the user [15]. The first one, Infrastructure as a Service (IaaS), mainly provides the lowest level of resource services, such as servers, storage, and networks. After enterprises or users rent these resources, they can customize their business systems according to their needs, which is considered the closest connection between people and machines and the equipment itself; the second one, Platform as a Service (PaaS), which is pre-built based on the second type, PaaS, is built on top of this with all the environment related to development, testing, operation, and maintenance. Individuals or enterprises can focus on their business logic and do not have to care about the underlying operating environment. The third type, Software as a Service (SaaS), is more straightforward, providing ready-made software or application services, such as email services. This is more universal in nature, as individuals and enterprises of any size need to use ready-made software of all kinds, providing a way for people to connect with various software facilities. SaaS provides a way for people to communicate with multiple software facilities. And on top of the user-based platform of data centers, certain connections exist between users and users and users and administrators.

The exchange of data between different users or companies through a pool of resources in a data center falls under the people-to-people (P2P) concept. The resource space provided by data centers can be divided into three categories according to how data centers resources are deployed [8]. The first category, the public cloud, refers to the vast number of users who rent help from the resource pool on demand to meet their needs [16]. Users pay for the actual resources they use over time. This model's ownership of the underlying resources belongs to the service provider, and the right to use them belongs to the customer. This reflects the sharing of resources in the resource pool by the users on the one hand and also the connection between the service provider and the customer. The second category, private cloud, refers to how some large enterprises structure themselves and deploy themselves self-sufficiently. It no longer shares the resource pool with all users. Still, it isolates the space resources for its use, which is well suited to the security operation and maintenance management of large enterprises.

The service and ownership of the underlying resources in this model belong to the customer. The third category, hybrid cloud, is a combination of the first two, where the cloud service provider helps you maintain your own cloud facilities or multi-cloud interoperability so that you can privatize the highly secure data and publicize the less essential parts, meeting security needs and saving costs, which is the mainstream deployment model at present [17]. These models embody the data exchange and connection between people through the internet in the Internet of Everything. In the Internet of Everything era, the relationship between people will be diversified and not limited to the initial physical contact, the connection is unavoidable, and the concept of the Internet of Everything can provide us with thoughts on how to find a suitable P2P approach. The idea of the Internet of Everything can provide us with a direction to think about how to find the right way of P2P.

For the existing M2M in the Internet of Things concept, there is more embodiment in data centers. On the one hand, from the perspective of the composition of data centers, the hardware of data centers is divided into two categories, namely, the leading and supporting equipment. Among them, the top equipment refers to the IT computing power equipment represented by the network and server, the communication equipment represented by switches, routers, and firewalls, and the supporting equipment refers to the underlying essential support equipment (such as power supply system and refrigeration system) to ensure the regular operation of the leading equipment, which are closely connected through data centers network to realize data interaction and collaborative work, which is the M2M concept in the Internet of Everything. Only when these machines and equipment are connected to their ability can they support the continuous operation of these massive data centers. On the other hand, as a single data center has been difficult to adapt to the business needs of the new era, the interconnection of data centers and data centers has also begun to be considered. To meet the cross-regional operation, user access, and the demand of the different disaster scenarios, more and more organizations and enterprises in other regions deployed multiple data centers in the same industry, and various industry enterprises often need data sharing and cooperation, which requires different enterprise connectivity between data centers [18]. The communication of data in other data centers is also a need for M2M in the Internet of Everything. In the Internet of Everything era, if the data is independent and unshared, and an effective connection needs to be established between different data centers, it is difficult for data centers to maintain their data storage and management advantages.

4   Development Trends of Data Centers and IoE

There are currently two dominant trends in data centers. One is to achieve interconnection between different data centers, as mentioned in Sect. 3. The number of data centers in the world today has proliferated, and the number of data centers is already large enough and widely distributed. However, how to achieve data exchange and sharing between data centers is now a significant consideration for mainstream data centers. From the Internet of Everything perspective, it is crucial to build on what was originally a relatively simple machine-to-machine connection for servers in close geographical proximity and develop it into a connection between different data centers across geographies. To meet data center interconnection requirements, Huawei CloudFabric Data Centre [19] relies on two key technologies, VXLAN and EVPN, to provide customers with a minimalist operational experience covering the entire lifecycle of cloud-based data center networks.

Second, it solves the energy consumption problem of data centers. According to the China "New Infrastructure" Development Research Report [8], data centers will account for the largest share of global energy consumption, up to 33%, by 2025, so how to save energy has become one of the issues on the minds of data centers today [20]. One is to choose a suitable environment for data center construction, such as subsea data centers or Arctic data centers, to save energy by using the environment to assist the cooling system. This not only keeps the energy required for cooling and heat dissipation but also widens the distribution of data centers, enabling the interconnection of everything through data centers [21]. The other is the intelligent management of the various facilities in data centers by monitoring the power consumption within the processor. This also embodies the interconnection between data centers, the environment, and humans.

5   Conclusion

From the history of data centers, the development of data centers is in line with the many ideas of the Internet of Everything; the development of data centers also complements the development of the Internet of Everything concept. The two have something in common. Judging from the current development of data centers, many existing service modes and construction methods of data centers are very compatible with the Internet of Everything P2M, P2P, and M2M. From the future trends of data centers, some of the existing future development directions are also very much in line with the Internet of Everything concept. We have reason to expect that the future of data centers will be better connected to the Internet of Everything concept, develop a new form of data centers, and the idea of the Internet of Everything.

References

1. Kiesler, N., Impagliazzo, J.: Perspectives on the internet of everything. In: Pereira, T., Impagliazzo, J., Santos, H. (eds) Internet of Everything. IoECon 2022. Lecture Notes of the Institute for Computer Sciences, Social Informatics and Telecommunications Engineering, vol. 458. Springer, Cham (2023). https://doi.org/10.1007/978-3-031-25222-8_1
2. Evans, D.: The Internet of Everything: How More Relevant and Valuable Connections Will Change the World. Cisco Internet Business Solutions Group (IBSG), Cisco Systems, Inc., San Jose, USA, White Paper (2012). https://www.cisco.com/c/dam/global/en_my/assets/cis coinnovate/pdfs/IoE.pdf
3. Moran, T.: The Internet of Everything. Online video presentation TEDx Talks (2021). https://youtu.be/K-FhMegdlJo
4. Lei, G., Fu, Y., Dongsheng, Liao, X.: Research on the development strategy of China's artificial intelligence core software and hardware. Strat. Study CAE **23**(3), 90–97 (2021)
5. Zhao, S., Chen, S.: Review and prospect of traffic identification technology based on machine learning. Comput. Eng. Sci. **40**(10), 1746–1756 (2018)
6. Balodis, R., Opmane, I.: History of data centre development. In: Tatnall, A. (ed.) Reflections on the History of Computing. IAICT, vol. 387, pp. 180–203. Springer, Heidelberg (2012). https://doi.org/10.1007/978-3-642-33899-1_13
7. Litton Power. Data Center Technology Trends for 2022
8. This article takes you through cloud computing. https://zhuanlan.zhihu.com/p/347589225
9. Weissberger, A.: TiECon 2014 Summary-Part 1: Qualcomm Keynote & IoT Track Overview (2014). https://techblog.comsoc.org/2014/05/23/tiecon-2014-summary-part-1-qua lcomm-keynote-iot-track-overview/
10. A brief discussion of data center network architecture. https://zhuanlan.zhihu.com/p/298 81248
11. Wu, H.: "Internet of Things Development Strategy Planning Research" consulting project comprehensive report foreign situation and general report. http://fx.gfkd.chaoxing.com/det ail_38502727e7500f261431eda37b8b94be924a13d0cf2815a71921b0a3ea255101f3886585 3bf86257fc80427a2ea1d4a409253634d05033b651b1d89c099d1ea071774a6ae86568b688d 4e2b13b9431f6
12. Ashton, K.: Internet of Everything vs. Internet of Things (2009). https://www.rfidjournal. com/that-internet-of-things-thing
13. Shinkarenko, A.: Internet of Everything vs. Internet of Things (2020). https://www.itrans ition.com/blog/internet-of-everything-vs-internet-of-things
14. Fenn, J., LeHong, H.: Hype cycle for emerging technologies 2011 (2011). https://www.gar tner.com/en/documents/1754719/hype-cycle-for-emerging-technologies-2011
15. Xie, R., Luo, W.: Data center development research. Electron. Technol. Softw. Eng. **12**, 185–187 (2019)
16. Yi, X., Liu, F., Niu, D., Jin, H., Lui, J.C.S.: Cocoa: dynamic container-based group buying strategies for cloud computing. ACM Trans. Model. Perf. Eval. Comput. Syst. **2**(2), 8 (2017). https://doi.org/10.1145/3022876
17. Xu, M., Toosi, A.N., Buyya, R.: A self-adaptive approach for managing applications and harnessing renewable energy for sustainable cloud computing. IEEE Trans. Sustain. Comput. **6**(4), 544–558 (2021). https://ieeexplore-ieee-org-s.libyc.nudt.edu.cn/stamp/stamp.jsp?tp=& arnumber=9162490

18. You, D., Lin, W., Shi, F., Li, J., Qi, D., Fong, S.: A novel approach for CPU load prediction of cloud server combining denoising and error correction. Computing **105**(3): 577–594 (2020). https://doi.org/10.1007/s00607-020-00865-y.pdf?pdf=button

19. A Report from Huawei about Data center interconnect. https://info.support.huawei.com/info-finder/encyclopedia/zh/%E6%95%B0%E6%8D%AE%E4%B8%AD%E5%BF%83%E4%BA%92%E8%81%94.html

20. Niu, Z., He, B., Liu, F.: JouleMR: towards cost-effective and green-aware data processing frameworks. IEEE Trans. Big Data **4**(2): 258–272 (2018). https://ieeexplore-ieee-org-s.libyc.nudt.edu.cn/stamp/stamp.jsp?tp=&arnumber=7827156

21. Lin, W., Wu, G., Wang, X.: An artificial neural network approach to power consumption model construction for servers in cloud data centers. IEEE Trans. Sustain. Comput. **5**(3), 329–340 (2020). https://ieeexplore-ieee-org-s.libyc.nudt.edu.cn/stamp/stamp.jsp?tp=&arnumber=8685195

Jamming LoRa and Evaluation of Ease of Implementation

Jonas Stenholt Melchior Jensen[1], Bjørn Alexander Wade Patterson[2],
Tomasz Blaszczyk[3]([✉]), and Birger Andersen[4]

[1] Cibicom, Ballerup, Denmark
[2] Danish Data Protection Agency, Valby, Denmark
[3] DIS Study Abroad in Scandinavia, Copenhagen, Denmark
tomb@dis.dk
[4] Technical University of Denmark, Kongens Lyngby, Denmark

Abstract. The number of wirelessly connected devices are on the rise.
With increasingly capable devices becoming cheaper and more accessible,
the threat towards these radio communications is steadily growing. One
of the more common technologies in the low power and long range realm
of these devices is LoRaWAN. With a selection of different readily available hardware, we have examined if it is possible to conduct jamming
attacks on LoRa. We have also evaluated the ease of implementation, and
found that it is possible for less technically proficient persons to carry
out effective jamming attacks on LoRa of different complexities using
affordable hardware and open-source software.

Keywords: LoRa · LPWAN · SDR · ESP32 · SODAQ ExpLoRer ·
Ettus USRP E312 · HackRF One · GNU Radio · Jamming

1 Introduction

The Internet of Things (IoT) as topic under Internet of Everything has attracted
much attention over the last years due to relevance in connecting devices all over
the world. Automation plays a large role in this, since homes and even entire
cities are looking to automate tedious tasks using the concept of IoT. A fundamental aspect of IoT is wireless communication technology whether short range
communication in home automation environments or long range communication
in larger scale IoT projects. Wireless Personal Area Networks (WPANs) such
as ZigBee, Bluetooth, or Z-wave and Wireless LANs (WLANs) such as WiFi all
provide for short range communication. When it comes to long range communication different technologies exist such as cellular communication, e.g., 5G, while
lower powered solutions such as Low Power Wireless Area Networks (LPWAN)
provide for longer battery life for end-devices with data rate as the trade off. An
overview of the different protocols can be seen in Fig. 1.

When researching different LPWANs, it becomes clear that the architecture
of the different protocols differ a lot both in terms of the PHYsical (PHY) layer,

T. Pereira et al. (Eds.): IOECON 2023, LNICST 551, pp. 19–41, 2024.
https://doi.org/10.1007/978-3-031-51572-9_3

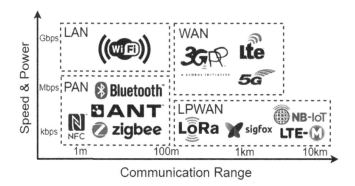

Fig. 1. Comparison of Wireless Protocols from [1].

Medium Access Control (MAC) layer and network layer. SigFox PHY is based on an ultra narrow band (200 Hz) and the entire network architecture is operated by SigFox (now unabiz), which means end users cannot deploy their own base stations/gateways and need to connect their end-devices to the SigFox back-end. In contrast to this, LoRa modulation [2] uses chirp spread spectrum utilizing a much wider frequency band, while LoRaWAN [3] allows for end users to deploy their own gateways and network servers which gives the opportunity to create private networks. Due to these features, LoRa has attracted a lot of attention and research on how to expand IoT environments [4,5], including in a context of sustainability [6].

With more data being transmitted via radio by IoT devices and these being used increasingly in sensitive/critical fields such as infrastructure monitoring, it is important to make sure that the focus on IT-security is continuous [7].

The concept of radio communication jamming encompasses a variety of methods designed to either interfere, disrupt or entirely block communications. These can be of low complexity such as random noise attacks or of a higher complexity such as a reactive attack. A simple Gaussian noise based attack is generally indiscriminate in nature. These attacks do not utilize any form of signal modulation, and are designed to blanket a selected frequency interval, interfering with the reception of the legitimate transmissions. For them to be effective, they often have to be continuous and high powered. This in turn makes it easier to track down and are often limited in their mobility due to need of a large power source. Reactive attacks are directed attacks that only act during a legitimate transmission. These jamming transmissions can also be modulated like the legitimate transmission, which can be more disruptive to technologies that work well in low Signal to Noise Ratio (SNR).

Electronic devices of a given capability generally decrease in price over time as technology advances. Along with the increased interest surrounding IoT implementation, this means that there are a lot of different IoT devices available to the public, including those with radio communication capabilities. This has the unintentional down side of making devices able to jam transmissions readily available to the public as well. Selecting the same or similar device to perform the attack allows for access to the used modulation, and the current availability makes getting a hold of them easy.

The evolution of Software Defined Radio (SDR) has resulted in a wide variety of cheap products that can quite easily be set-up by lower skilled technical persons, for analysis of any transmission that they encounter. Devices such as the Great Scott Gadgets HackRF One are able to operate between 1MHz to 6GHz which covers most of the bands used by devices in the realm of IoT [8] and even technologies such as WiFi. These devices play a large role in the implementation of jamming methods, as they can be used as the main tool for determining the parameters of a given signal, of which the jamming methods can be tuned towards. They can also perform attacks themselves, as some of them also have transmitting capabilities.

In our work we evaluate the ease-of-implementation regarding being able to perform jamming attacks on legitimate LoRa PHY layer transmissions. This is done with the help of an array of set-ups using different publicly available hardware (IoT devices and SDRs) and jamming techniques of various complexities. We also discus the potential security impacts this may have on the current IoT landscape.

2 Background

In the following sections, an explanation of LoRa PHY and LoRaWAN principles will be provided. Prior work regarding jamming attacks on LoRa PHY will also be discussed.

2.1 LoRa PHY

At the physical layer LoRa uses its own modulation technique maintained by Semtech [2], based on Chirp Spread Spectrum (CSS). A chirp can be characterized as a sinusoidal wave, which either increases (up-chirp) or decreases (down-chirp) linearly over time in the frequency spectrum. In Fig. 2, a chirp in the time domain is visualized. Note that this is how the modulated signal in CSS will look in time domain.

What LoRa does differently is that the frequency shifting depends on the symbol transmitted which adds discontinuity to the modulated signal in the time domain. A thorough mathematical description of LoRa modulation was introduced in [9], which also raises the idea that LoRa might be better described as Frequency Shift Chirp Modulation (FSCM). The modulated signal c is expressed as

$$c = \frac{1}{\sqrt{2^{SF}}} e^{i2\pi[(s(nT_s)+k)2^{SF}]kT\frac{B}{2^{SF}}}$$

where SF is the spreading factor and the number of possible symbols is $2^{SF} - 1$. The symbol to be transmitted is represented as $s(nT_s)$ where T_s is the period of transmitting one full symbol. What is worth noticing, is that the frequency is in

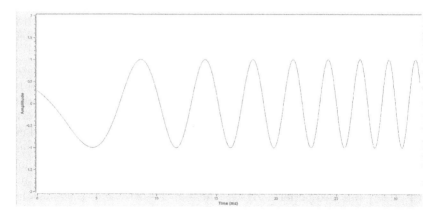

Fig. 2. A chirp in time domain.

fact increasing linearly with k as the time index. A discontinuity is introduced in term 2^{SF}, hence the name frequency shift chirp modulation. These features can bee seen in Fig. 3, where the symbol dictates the starting frequency, after which it increases linearly until it reaches the bandwidth limit and then returns to the lowest frequency within the given bandwidth increasing to the starting frequency again.

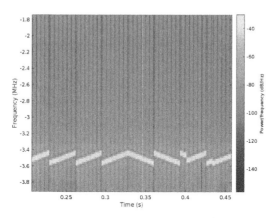

Fig. 3. LoRa chirps in frequency domain.

From [2] we have bit rate R_b on the output of the modulator expressed as

$$R_b = SF \cdot \frac{1}{\frac{2^{SF}}{BW}}$$

where BW is the modulation bandwidth in Hz. What can be derived from this, is that with a larger spreading factor of a given bandwidth (usually 125 KHz in LoRa), the bit rate decreases, meaning longer transmission times for larger spreading factors which is a key property of LoRa.

What happens at the receiving end of LoRa, is that to detect an incoming signal, the transmitter will send a preamble usually of 8 up-chirps followed by the actual data symbols. To demodulate the signal, it is first multiplied by an inverse chirp resulting in constant frequencies of the symbols. Conceptually after "de-chirping", a similarity check is performed between the received symbols and the base symbols representing perfect chirp representations of the different symbols. The functionality of this is performed by Discrete Time Fourier Transform (DTFT) - in most receiver designs Fast Fourier Transform (FFT), which outputs the signal in frequency domain to be correlated with the frequency components of the base chirps. The most significant frequencies output by FFT, represent the transmitted symbols at least for low noise levels. Figure 4 illustrates exactly this, where DTFT is performed on a de-chirped signal in which the highest amplitudes of the different frequency components will be considered the frequencies of the de-chirped transmitted symbols.

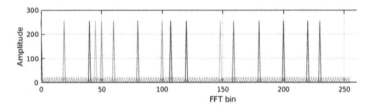

Fig. 4. LoRa FFT [10].

CSS (and DTFT) is a part of the explanation on why LoRa is robust against high noise levels and can even be demodulated from below the noise floor due to exactly this correlation check. As an example, with a spreading factor of 12 reliable communication can be achieved at SNR of −20 dB. In fact you can have a link budget of approximately 151 dB for a spreading factor of 12 with the receiver sensitivity being −137 dBm. A complete list of the link budget for the different spreading factor with a bandwidth of 125 kHz and fixed transmission power can be seen in Table 1 from [2].

Table 1. Link budget for different spreading factors in LoRa.

Mode	Equivalent bit rate (kb/s)	Sensitivity (dBm)
LoRa SF = 12	0.293	−137
LoRa SF = 11	0.537	−134.5
LoRa SF = 10	0.976	−132
LoRa SF = 9	1757	−129.7
LoRa SF = 8	3125	−126
LoRa SF = 7	5468	−123

2.2   LoRaWAN

LoRaWAN is the network protocol present in the MAC layer specified in [3]. The general architecture of a LoRaWAN network can be seen in Fig. 5 where different end-devices communicate with gateways using LoRa on the physical level. The gateways are connected to a network server through the TCP/IP protocol (secured by TLS) which has the responsibility of sending the payloads to various applications. Payload is further secured end-to-end by AES encryption.

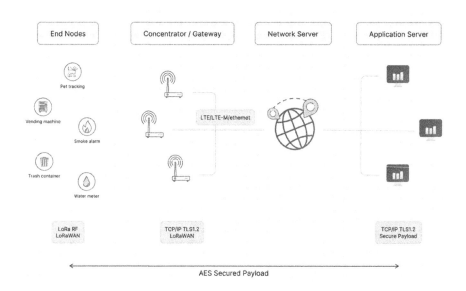

Fig. 5. LoRaWAN architecture [11].

One of the major delimiters of this specification is the different device classes where an end-device can either be of class A, B or C. Uplink communication is labeled as communication from end-device to network server while downlink communication is labeled as communication from network server to end-device. Class A is the least power consuming, since each device only listens for downlink messages during two receive windows after each uplink transmission (RX1 and RX2). For class B devices, the gateways within the network will synchronously broadcast a beacon which is the reference used by end-devices to open receive windows periodically synchronized with exactly these beacon signals. Class C devices will continuously listen for downlink traffic when not transmitting, being the most power consuming class.

For a device to be activated, i.e., joined to network, there are two methods of activation - Activation By Personalization (ABP) and Over-The-Air Activation (OTAA). In general OTAA is recommended, since it depends on the derivation of AES keys rather than fixed hard coded keys in the end-device as in ABP as specified in [3]. In LoRaWAN 1.1, 5 keys are derived from two root keys, AppKey (Application key) and NwkKey (Network Key) which are assigned to the end-device during fabrication (in case of ABP). From NwkKey, 3 network session keys are derived: FNwkSIntKey, SNwkSIntKey and NwkSEncKey. From AppKey, 1 application session key is derived: AppSKey. All keys are AES-128 symmetric keys where the network session keys are used for integrity check from end-device to network server using AES-128 CMAC mode while the application session key is used for confidentiality from end-device to application server using AES-128 CTR mode. In prior versions to LoRaWAN 1.1, only two sessions keys were derived: Network session key (NwkSKey) and application session key (AppSKey).

An important consideration for LoRaWAN networks are the duty cycles associated with the license-free bands regulated in [12], which specifies how many times a device may transmit per time unit. In EU863-870, the duty cycles are specified for 5 sub-bands depicted in Table 2. All radio devices in the network must follow these constraints to be compliant with LoRaWAN, i.e., both end-devices and gateways. Some end-devices have radio modules which enforce the duty cycles automatically and will throw error messages if a duty in a given sub-band is exceeded.

Table 2. Duty cycles in EU863-870.

Bands	Duty cycles
Sub-band 1 (863.0–868.0 MHz)	1%
Sub-band 2 (868.0–868.6 MHz)	1%
Sub-band 3 (868.7–869.2 MHz)	0.1%
Sub-band 4 (869.4–869.65 MHz)	10%
Sub-band 5 (869.7–870.0 MHz)	1%

Table 3. Frequency Plans for TTN.

Frequency (MHz)	SF and bandwidth delimiters
868.1	SF7BW125 to SF12BW125
868.3	SF7BW125 to SF12BW125 and SF7BW250
868.5	SF7BW125 to SF12BW125
867.1	SF7BW125 to SF12BW125
867.3	SF7BW125 to SF12BW125
867.5	SF7BW125 to SF12BW125
867.7	SF7BW125 to SF12BW125
867.9	SF7BW125 to SF12BW125
868.8	SFK
869.525	SF9BW125 (RX2)

The different channel frequencies used in LoRaWAN depend on the community network, however compliant with the LoRaWAN regional parameters [13]. The network used in this project for testing purposes is The Things Network (TTN), which also specify the channel frequencies in EU863-870, depicted in Table 3. Note that the channel used for downlink communication in RX1, is a function of the channel and data rate used in the initial uplink transmission.

2.3   LoRa Jamming

Due to the demodulation scheme, LoRa is robust to interference and noise. In [14], jamming with Gaussian noise was possible at the expense of transmission power and demonstrated that LoRa PHY is robust to noise compared to other wireless technologies. In [7] was simulated a scenario in which the jamming device and legitimate device were placed 500 m and 2000 m away respectively from the gateway and Package Error Rates (PERs) above 10^{-1} was achieved using a Gaussian noise source with the jamming node only transmitting at 40% compared to the power of the legitimate node.

In [16,17] is shown that simultaneous LoRa transmissions with same frequency and spreading factor can collide with each other and not be resolved. A premise for this is that the jamming chirps must have a higher transmission power than the legitimate ones [15]. In such a scenario, the FFT performed in a given demodulation window would result in the jamming chirps having higher amplitudes rendering the legitimate chirps invalid. This jamming technique was utilized in [18] using commercial off-the-shelf LoRa devices. In [14] is suggested a similar approach in which the chirps also should be well aligned in the time domain and mimic legitimate chirps in the frequency domain to bypass collision recovery methods such as [19]. In order to align the chirps well and perform effective jamming with low probability of detection, reactive jamming is often sufficient which is also tested in [18]. The general setup for such an approach is to scan for a LoRa preamble with a specific spreading factor on a specific channel. Since most end-devices only allow for scanning a single channel for a preamble with a certain spreading factor at a time, channel hopping can be deployed as in [20], sequentially scanning channels to detect the preamble after which the jamming signal will be transmitted.

For our study, 4 jamming techniques derived from above discoveries will be used:

1. *Single Channel jamming (SC):* Jamming with LoRa modulation on one channel, transmitting continuously with a fixed spreading factor.
2. *Channel Hopping jamming (CH):* Jamming with LoRa modulation in which jamming device will jump between the channels (downlink) specified in Table 3 with a fixed spreading factor.
3. *Reactive Jamming (RJ):* The jamming device will utilize channel hopping when listening for a preamble on all downlink channel frequencies with a fixed spreading factor and start transmitting a LoRa signal when the preamble has been detected.
4. *Gaussian Noise jamming (GN):* The noise floor will be raised, such that the legitimate transmitted LoRa symbols can not be demodulated.

In an attempt to jam LoRa PHY, different experimental setups have been used. SDRs provide a great analytical tool and also have the capability of jamming with different RF signals as opposed to a standard LoRa only module. In [14,21], SDRs were used with the GNU Radio open-source software where the jamming signals were implemented. When going for an on-board LoRa module and Micro Controller (MCU), the SX127x LoRa module is popular and has good library support. In [22] was deployed an ESP32 embedded with an SX1276 module and [20] used an Arduino UNO connected to an external SX1276 module - In both cases, SX1276 with MCU acting as the jamming devices.

3   Materials and Methods

To test our selection of hardware's ability to jam LoRa transmissions, we set up a LoRa end-device to send legitimate join requests and data transmissions to a LoRa gateway, and attempted to jam them (Table 4).

Table 4. List of utilized hardware.

Module	Action	Modes
SODAQ ExpLoRer (RN2483 [23])	Transmitter	fixed SF12
Kerlink Wirnet iFemtoCell indoor LoRaWAN Gateway	Receiver	–
Great Scott Gadgets HackRF One [8]	Jammer	SC
ESP32 [24] with SX1276 [25]	Jammer	SC, CH, RJ
Ettus Research USRP E312 [26]	Jammer	GN

The jamming transmissions were all LoRa CSS signals at the same spreading factor as the legitimate transmissions. Both the legitimate LoRa end-device and LoRaWAN gateway were registered at on TTN, allowing us to track received transmissions (feature provided by TTN).

3.1   SODAQ ExpLoRer

The SODAQ ExpLoRer board was our real-world end-device analogue, used to send all transmissions during our experiments. To increase the chances of collision during our test and experiments, we forced the board to transmit using spreading factor 12. This would give us transmission times of up to 1500 ms depending on payload size [18], giving us more time to react and a better ability to follow jamming attempts visually, via a waterfall viewer in the AngelSDR software. In our case our payload was a single incremental digit, representing the number of the transmission (0–6). We used sub-band 1, described in Fig. 2. This was done with a simple c++ program, using the Sodaq_RN2483 library[1].

---

[1] www.github.com/SodaqMoja/Sodaq_RN2483, accessed on the 15th of January 2023.

These configuration changes were made for practicality reasons, but we believe that our source of legitimate transmissions is close enough to a real world implementation for us to assess the real world application of our techniques. The transmission power was set using an inbuilt function, and was set to a value of 5, equalling a transmission power of below 14 dBm = 25.12 mW. This is the lowest transmission power available for use on the 868 MHz band [23]. OTAA was used as the activation method during all tests and experiments. Due to duty cycle compliance we had a limit on how often we could transmit our legitimate LoRa transmissions. This resulted in us only being able to send up to 7 data transmissions after each successful join-request. For practicality reasons and time constraints we used this limit as the basis for how many transmissions we would send per set during our experiments.

The end-device was set up in such a way, that if it experienced 3 failed join requests, the program would halt stopping further attempts.

3.2 HackRF One

For the HackRF One jamming implementation, GNU Radio was utilized to implement SDR. Since we are using LoRa signals to jam LoRa PHY for this device, a GNU Radio SDR LoRa transceiver implementation [27] was used to generate our jamming LoRa signals. To connect the HackRF One to GNU Radio, we used Osmocom blocks from the library[2]. The block diagram used in our experiments can be seen in Fig. 6 in which SC jamming with center frequency 867.3 MHz was performed.

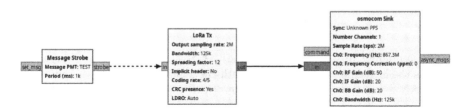

Fig. 6. HackRF One GNU Radio jamming SC implementation.

3.3 ESP32 with SX1276 LoRa Module

For the ESP32 embedded with an SX1276 LoRa module, several LoRa libraries were used in relation to the different jamming techniques.

---

[2] www.github.com/osmocom/gr-osmosdr, accessed on the 19th of January 2023.

SC Implementation. For the *SC* jamming implementation, an Arduino library[3] for the SX1276 was used to transmit LoRa signals on the frequency 867.1 MHz for this implementation. The associated code can be seen below in Listing 1 where the Serial Peripheral Interface (SPI) between the ESP32 and SX1276 module is established and the LoRa PHY parameters are set afterwards.

```
1   #include <SPI.h>
2   #include <LoRa.h>
3
4   // Pinout to SX1276
5   #define SCK 5
6   #define MISO 19
7   #define MOSI 27
8   #define SS 18
9   #define RST 14
10  #define DIO0 26
11
12  #define BAND 867.1E6
13
14  int frequency = BAND;
15
16  void setup() {
17    //SPI interface to SX1276
18    SPI.begin(SCK, MISO, MOSI, SS);
19    //setup SX1276
20    LoRa.setPins(SS, RST, DIO0);
21
22    if (!LoRa.begin(BAND)) {
23      while (1);
24    }
25
26    LoRa.setFrequency(frequency);
27    LoRa.setSpreadingFactor(12);
28    LoRa.setTxPower(14);
29    LoRa.setSignalBandwidth(125E3);
30    delay(2000);
31  }
32
33  void loop() {
34    LoRa.beginPacket();
```

---

[3] www.github.com/sandeepmistry/arduino-LoRa, accessed on the 18th january 2023.

```
35    LoRa.print("jamming");
36    LoRa.endPacket();
37  }
```

Listing 1. SC Source Code.

CH Implementation. For the *CH* jamming implementation, the same library as in *SC* was used. The way channel hopping can be achieved is simply by incrementing the center frequency by 0.2 MHz and make sure, that we do not exceed the bands specified in Table 3. The only changes made to the code is in the loop function (Listing 2).

```
1   void loop() {
2     // Wrap around
3     if (frequency == 868.7E6) {
4       frequency = BAND;
5     }
6
7     LoRa.setFrequency(frequency);
8
9     LoRa.beginPacket();
10    LoRa.print("jamming");
11    LoRa.endPacket();
12
13    frequency += 0.2E6;
14  }
```

Listing 2. CH Source Code - setup equivalent to Listing 1.

RJ Implementation. For reactive jamming, RadioLib was used[4] which has preamble detection functionality for the SX1276. The code written for this implementation can be seen in Listing 3, where channel hopping again is utilized in the sense that the SX1276 is listening sequentially on all channels in the band and transmits whenever a preamble is detected.

```
1   #include <RadioLib.h>
2
3   #define LORA_SCK     05
4   #define LORA_MISO    19
5   #define LORA_MOSI    27
```

---

[4] https://github.com/jgromes/RadioLib, accessed on the 21st January.

```
 6   #define LORA_SS        18
 7   #define LORA_DIO0      26
 8   #define LORA_DIO1      33
 9   #define LORA_RST       14
10
11   float frequency =      867.1;
12
13   SX1276 radio = new Module(LORA_SS, LORA_DIO0, LORA_RST, LORA_DIO1);
14
15   void setup() {
16
17     // Setup SX1276 wiring to ESP32
18     int state = radio.begin();
19     if (state != RADIOLIB_ERR_NONE) {
20       while (true);
21     }
22
23     radio.setPreambleLength(8);
24     radio.setOutputPower(14);
25     radio.setCodingRate(5);
26     radio.setSpreadingFactor(12);
27     radio.setSyncWord(34);
28     radio.setGain(1);
29
30     delay(100);
31   }
32
33   void loop() {
34     radio.setFrequency(frequency);
35
36     if (radio.scanChannel() == RADIOLIB_PREAMBLE_DETECTED) {
37       radio.transmit("");
38       delay(100);
39     }
40     frequency = frequency + 0.2;
41     if (frequency > 868.5) {
42       frequency = 867.1;
43     }
44   }
```

Listing 3. RJ Source Code.

3.4   Ettus USRP E312

For the Ettus USRP E312, many possibilities exist regarding how to transmit the jamming signal. Since it runs an embedded OS, it has built-in commands which can generate different signals. A more popular and common approach is however to develop the program on a host PC usually in GNU Radio and connect the USRP through the UHD driver, which needs to be of at least version 4.0 on host and target. The GNU Radio implementation with a Gaussian noise source can be seen in Fig. 7.

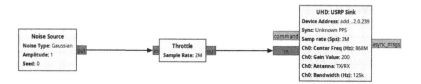

Fig. 7. USRP E312 Gnu Radio jamming *GN* implementation.

3.5   Experimental Methonds and Set-Ups

Each experiment consisted of three local devices: The legitimate transmitter (SODAQ ExpLoRer), the receiver (Kerlink LoRaWAN Gateway) and the jamming device and the LoRaWAN network and application server (TTN) which allowed for monitoring.

The experiments were performed indoor at with a static set-up. For all SC, CH and RJ experiments, there was approximately 57 m direct line-of-sight between the SODAQ transmitter and the gateway, and the jammer was approximately 2 m from the gateway. Along the transmission path the signal passed through an interior wall and an interior floor. For the GN experiment, there was approximately 47 m direct line-of-sight between the SODAQ transmitter and the gateway, and the jammer was approximately 1 m from the gateway. Along the transmission path the signal passed through 2 exterior walls.

To determine if a transmission was successfully jammed we used the live data feed from TTN. This displays the up- and down-links from the LoRaWAN application server. We visually confirmed new entries in the list to determine if the data transmission had made it through or not. The number of outgoing transmissions was counted in the software on the SODAQ board and printed to screen via a serial monitor, and we also visually confirmed that the transmission was put on the air. This was done by monitoring the waterfall visualisation of the sub-band in AngelSDR using a HackRF One as a receiver. Comparing the number of logged outgoing transmissions versus the number of received transmissions on the application server, we could calculate a jamming rate (Fig. 8):

$$\frac{jammed\ tx}{total\ tx} \cdot 100 = jamming\ rate\%$$

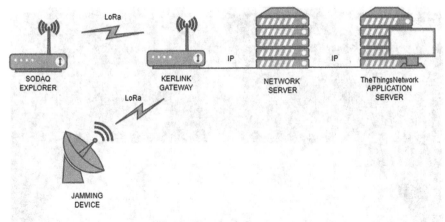

Fig. 8. Test bed diagram.

Our tests consisted of 7 sets of 7 transmissions. The first 5 sets of 7 were performed with the jamming device active, and the final 2 acted as a control, with the jamming device turned off. If the test resulted in a jamming rate > 0% it would validate our jamming technique as a successful proof-of-concept. If a jamming device was so effective as to block all join-request attempts, we would limit that set to the 3 join-request attempts the SODAQ board would attempt before halting. As join requests default to a spreading factor of 12, this lined up with the fixed spreading factor used as a fixed value throughout our experiments.

4   Experimental Results

As mentioned before, the jamming techniques (exceptGaussian noise) are based on jamming LoRa with LoRa. What this looks like in practice can be seen in Fig. 9 where the chirps with highest amplitude (yellow) are the jamming signal and overlaps with the legitimate chirps (green). Note that the jamming signal in fact mimics the legitimate signal both with spreading factor and channel center frequency while occupying close to the exact bandwidth of the legitimate signal.

When jamming with Gaussian noise as the source, Fig. 10 shows the most significant frequency components overlapping with the center frequency of LoRa channels in Table 3, which did in fact jam the communication.

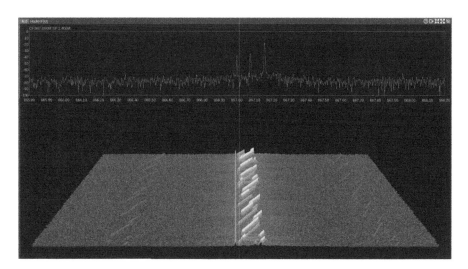

Fig. 9. Jamming LoRa with LoRa, captured with HackRF One in AngelSDR. (Color figure online)

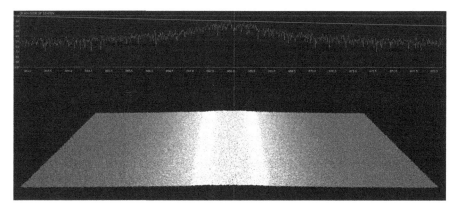

Fig. 10. Jamming LoRa with Gaussian noise, captured with HackRF One in AngelSDR. (Color figure online)

4.1   Jamming Results

Here we present the jamming results in Tables 5, 6, 7, 8, and 9. Note that all jamming devices' transmission power are at 14 dBm. All experiments consisted of 7 data transmission attempts, after a successful join-request attempt except for the experiments with the ESP32 and E312. Due to the effectiveness of the jamming techniques, we were not able to perform a successful join-request. Therefore the 3 join-request attempts are noted instead.

Table 5. HackRF One, Single Channel jamming results.

Run	Type	Jamming Rate
#1	Jamming	$1/7 \approx 14\%$
#2	Jamming	$2/7 \approx 29\%$
#3	Jamming	$2/7 \approx 29\%$
#4	Jamming	$1/7 \approx 14\%$
#5	Jamming	$1/7 \approx 14\%$
#6	Control	$0/7 = 0\%$
#7	Control	$0/7 = 0\%$

Table 6. ESP32 with SX1276, Single Channel jamming results.

Run	Type	Jamming Rate
#1	Jamming	$1/7 \approx 14\%$
#2	Jamming	$1/7 \approx 14\%$
#3	Jamming	$1/7 \approx 14\%$
#4	Jamming	$1/7 \approx 14\%$
#5	Jamming	$1/7 \approx 14\%$
#6	Control	$0/7 = 0\%$
#7	Control	$0/7 = 0\%$

Table 7. ESP32 with SX1276, Channel Hopping jamming results.

Run	Type	Jamming Rate
#1	Jamming	$2/7 \approx 29\%$
#2	Jamming	$2/7 \approx 29\%$
#3	Jamming	$3/7 \approx 43\%$
#4	Jamming	$1/7 \approx 14\%$
#5	Jamming	$1/7 \approx 14\%$
#6	Control	$0/7 = 0\%$
#7	Control	$0/7 = 0\%$

Table 8. ESP32 with SX1276, Channel Hopping jamming results.

Run	Type	Jamming Rate
#1	Jamming	$3/3 = 100\%$
#2	Jamming	$3/3 = 100\%$
#3	Jamming	$3/3 = 100\%$
#4	Jamming	$3/3 = 100\%$
#5	Jamming	$3/3 = 100\%$
#6	Control	$0/7 = 0\%$
#7	Control	$0/7 = 0\%$

Table 9. USRP E312, Gaussian Noise jamming results.

Run	Type	Jamming Rate
#1	Jamming	$3/3 = 100\%$
#2	Jamming	$3/3 = 100\%$
#3	Jamming	$3/3 = 100\%$
#4	Jamming	$3/3 = 100\%$
#5	Jamming	$3/3 = 100\%$
#6	Control	$0/7 = 0\%$
#7	Control	$0/7 = 0\%$

5 Discussions

As can be seen in the jamming experiment results, SC both the HackRF and ESP32 with SX1276 jammed approximately one packet in every run. This relates to the fact that LoRaWAN utilizes pseudo-random channel hopping to avoid collisions, which is why one could expect a jamming rate of approximately $1/8$ (8 downlink channels in Table 3), provided that continuous transmission is performed by the jamming device. CH jamming using the ESP32 with SX1276 performed a little better due to the fact that an ongoing legitimate transmission sometimes partially collides with a jamming signal. As expected, the RC jamming results gave a 100% jamming rate since the method is based on jamming the exact channel, the legitimate device is transmitting on whenever a preamble is detected. The simpler approach of GN jamming also resulted in a 100% jamming rate since the legitimate chirps were submerged by the Gaussian noise at such a level that the de-modulation was not able to distinguish the legitimate transmission.

It should be stated that SC, CH and GN jamming techniques all are easily detectable since they all exceed the regulated duty cycles and all use continuous transmission with no random element, at least in our implementation. A point worth raising is also, that jamming is indeed a malicious action and bypassing regional restrictions might not be of great significance to the adversary, rather the probability of being detected. RJ is on the contrary a much more careful technique. Since the jamming transmissions overlap with the legitimate transmissions and in our case mimic the exact channel and bandwidth of the legitimate signal, they are much harder to detect.

5.1 Countermeasures

To avoid jamming and in general minimize the chance of collision in LoRaWAN, a good approach is to utilize Adaptive Data Rate (ADR), meaning end-devices will vary their SF, bandwidth and transmission power in order to optimize data rate and energy consumption and ensuring that gateways can demodulate the transmitted signals. For a lot of jamming implementations including ours, ADR is in fact sufficient to establish decent communication since a fixed spreading factor is used for the jamming device. ADR combined with channel hopping for legitimate devices limits jamming possibilities, since the range of channel frequencies for every spreading factor need to be iterated when jamming, whether *CH* or *RJ* is deployed.

In general, it is a good idea to look into the default behavior of an end-device and the libraries used to program it. Not all end-devices use channel hopping and ADR by default which sometimes have to be implemented by the user. Furthermore, ADR has to be implemented in LoRaWAN and if an end-device is not connected to a bigger community network such as, e.g., TTN, ADR might not be available, since it is the responsibility of the network server to indicate whether lower or higher data rates should be used.

More targeted countermeasures do however also exist. In [19] is proposed a parallel decoding technique (FTrack) for simultaneous LoRa transmissions at same frequency and same SF utilizing the fact, that the chirps might be and often are slightly misaligned in time domain. Hardware imperfections might also result in two simultaneous transmission differ slightly in frequency, where [28] (Choir) uses exactly these differences in frequency to distinguish different signals from each other.

5.2 Board Accessibility

The SODAQ ExpLoRer, HackRF One and ESP32 devices are all sub $500, as of January 2023, and we evaluate that they can be used by persons with slightly above average technical knowledge and skills. They all can be programmed and deployed with a consumer grade laptop/desktop computer. The software necessary to program them, such as Arduino IDE, GNU Radio, AngelSDR and the code libraries mentioned in the article are all free and open source. We evaluate that amount and quality of supportive material online, in the form of step-by-step guides on sites such as YouTube.com, GitHub.com and StackOverflow.com, is very high. This allows users to implement jamming capabilities, without deep technical knowledge of the underlying maths or physics. We believe that the average person interested in executing the attacks that we have demonstrated would have the skills to perform them.

The Ettus USRP E312 retails at around $5,000, as of January 2023, and we believe the price makes this device less accessible to the average person, compared to the devices mentioned above. For a person to use this device effectively, we believe that they will need a good understanding of UNIX type operating systems, local area networking, serial communication, radio communication and potentially the compilation of necessary software and drivers. The supportive material online is of a higher technical complexity, making it difficult to work with. Based on these assumptions we believe that this device requires at least the equivalent technical knowledge of a second year technical university student to program and implement as a LoRa jamming device.

5.3 Evaluation of Ease of Implementation

For the array of jamming devices used in our test setups it is relevant to make a high level evaluation on the difficulty of implementing these devices in practise. In relation to above explanation and experiences when implementing the devices' functionalities, we came up with Table 10[5]. The configuration parameter encapsulates installation of software implementation of, e.g., GNU Radio LoRa transceiver functionality [27], required UNIX experience, and in general tweaks needed to perform the jamming. Note that programming might be relevant on the HackRF and USRP, but a more popular approach is however to utilize GNU Radio functionality, which is why we rendered this parameter as *N/A* for these

Table 10. Evaluation of ease of implementation.

Device	Configuration	Programming	Flexibility	Compat.	Price
HackRF One	Medium	N/A	Medium High	Low	Low
ESP32 + SX1276	Easy	Easy	Low	High	Low
USRP E312	Hard	N/A	High	Low	High

devices in an adversary use-case. Flexibility denotes how flexible the devices are in terms of different jamming types which of course has to be compatible with the radio module in the devices. For both of the SDRs any signal can really be generated and the USRP E312 has enough transmission power and bandwidth to generate sufficient noise to jam LoRa communication. It might seem ambiguous, that the ESP32 with SX1276 has low flexibility, since we conducted both *SC, CH* and *RJ* for this device, but in the context of jamming with different signals, the SX1276 is indeed a LoRa module only able to jam LoRa with LoRa. Jamming LoRa with LoRa however, seems like the most efficient method also suggested in previous work, which is why the ESP32 with SX1276 is an easy to setup and efficient jammer in this context. The SDRs are however not as compatible with LoRa PHY, since external implementations of LoRa in GNU Radio need to be installed and configured.

As an overall assessment, everything taken into consideration, we have ranked the three devices in terms of the easiest jammer to implement against LoRa PHY in an adversary use-case:

1. ESP32 with SX1276
2. HackRF One
3. Ettus USRP E312

6 Conclusions

As more and more LPWAN capable devices are being fielded, and devices are being trusted with more sensitive tasks, the security surrounding these systems

---

[5] "Compat." means compatibility in terms of LoRa PHY.

must not lag behind. The LoRa protocol is very resilient towards low SNR and simultaneous transmissions of non LoRa modulation. However, it is not immune towards attacks utilizing the same type of CSS modulation.

We have put together 4 combinations of hardwares and jamming approaches to demonstrate this fact. With these experiments we have demonstrated that it is easy for a hostile actor to mount a LoRa jamming attack using cheap and readily available hardware, adding these to the already existing pool of more capable but also more expensive hardware. These range from a disruption of singular transmissions to a full DoS attack. Without much work a jamming attack can be improved to become a reactive attack, which is a lot more clandestine in nature. These types of attacks have a higher success rate, as the randomized nature of trying to catch a channel hopping signal is removed. We believe that due to the availability and low level of technical knowledge needed to perform such attacks, we could see a rise of LoRa device attacks in the future. If these devices are used as a part of infrastructural systems, this could have devastating results.

7 Future Work

The legitimate transmitter in our experiments was limited to the use of spreading factor 12, for practical reasons. One can argue that our analogue of an average LoRaWAN end-device is not truly representative of the targets an hostile actor would encounter in the field. A continuation of the work where the end-device is subjected to ADR, and other such methods of signal optimization, is required to be sure that our methods would still be viable. A more rigorous set of experiments with a larger set of parameters, such as more spreading factors, channels, signal powers, etc., should be realized.

The reactive attack could be extended to include an element of selectivity, seeking out only to jam transmissions from a specific end-device. This would raise the difficulty of detection even further, making fixing the situation that much harder. This type of attack would need a slightly deeper knowledge of the inner workings of the LoRa packet composition, but this information is readily available, and does not require a large leap in technical understanding to learn.

References

1. Jiang, X., et al.: Hybrid low-power wide-area mesh network for IoT applications. IEEE Internet Things J. **8**(2), 901–915 (2021)
2. AN1200.22 LoRa^{TM} Modulation Basics. https://www.frugalprototype.com/wp-content/uploads/2016/08/an1200.22.pdf. Accessed 15 Jan 2023
3. LoRaWAN^{TM} 1.1 Specification. https://hz137b.p3cdn1.secureserver.net/wp-content/uploads/2020/11/lorawantm_specification_-v1.1.pdf?time=1673563697. Accessed 15 Jan 2023
4. Msaad, M., Hambly, A., Mariani, P., Kosta, S.: Mobile and delay tolerant network for LoRa at sea. In: CoNEXT 2020: Proceedings of the Student Workshop. ACM (2020)

5. Fargas, B., Petersen, M.: GPS-free geolocation using LoRa in low-power WANs. In: GIoTS 2017 - Global Internet of Things Summit, Proceedings (2017)
6. Orfanidis, C., Dimitrakopoulos, K., Fafoutis, X., Jacobsson, M.: Towards battery-free LPWAN wearables. In: ENSsys 2019 - Proceedings of the 7th International Workshop on Energy Harvesting and Energy-Neutral Sensing Systems, pp. 52–53 (2019)
7. Prasad, N., Lynggaard, P.: LoRaWan sensitivity analysis and prevention strategies against wireless DoS attacks. Wirel. Pers. Commun. **126**, 3663–3675 (2022). https://doi.org/10.1007/s11277-022-09884-8
8. Great Scott Gadgets, HackRF One specification. https://hackrf.readthedocs.io/en/latest/index.html. Accessed 15 Jan 2023
9. Vangelista, L.: Frequency shift chirp modulation: the LoRa modulation. IEEE Sig. Process. Lett. **24**, 1818–1821 (2017)
10. Liando, J., Jg, A., Tengourtius, A., Li, M.: Known and unknown facts of LoRa: experiences from a large-scale measurement study. ACM Trans. Sens. Netw. **15**, 1–35 (2019)
11. LoRaWAN architecture. https://www.thethingsnetwork.org/docs/lorawan/architecture/. Accessed 21 Jan 2023
12. ETSI En 300 220-1 V3.1.1. https://www.etsi.org/deliver/etsi_en/300200_300299/30022001/03.01.01_60/en_30022001v030101p.pdf. Accessed 18 Jan 2023
13. RP2-1.0.3 LoRaWAN® Regional Parameters. https://hz137b.p3cdn1.secureserver.net/wp-content/uploads/2021/05/RP002-1.0.3-FINAL-1.pdf?time=1674070505. Accessed 18 Jan 2023
14. Hou, N., Xia, X., Zheng, Y.: Jamming of LoRa PHY and countermeasure. In: Proceedings - IEEE INFOCOM (2021)
15. Hou, N., Xia, X., Zheng, Y.: Jamming of LoRa PHY and countermeasure. ACM Trans. Sens. Netw. **19**(4), 1–27 (2023). Article No. 80
16. Reynders, B., Meert, W., Pollin, S.: Range and coexistence analysis of long range unlicensed communication. In: 2016 23rd International Conference On Telecommunications, ICT (2016)
17. Aras, E., Small, N., Ramachandran, G., Delbruel, S., Joosen, W., Hughes, D.: Selective jamming of LoRaWAN using commodity hardware. In: ACM International Conference Proceeding Series, pp. 363–372 (2017)
18. Aras, E., Ramachandran, G., Lawrence, P., Hughes, D.: Exploring the security vulnerabilities of LoRa. In: 2017 3rd IEEE International Conference on Cybernetics (CYBCONF), pp. 1–6 (2017)
19. Xia, X., Zheng, Y., Gu, T.: FTrack: parallel decoding for LoRa transmissions. IEEE/ACM Trans. Networking **28**, 2573–2586 (2020)
20. Perković, T., Rudeš, H., Damjanović, S., Nakić, A.: Low-cost implementation of reactive jammer on LoRaWAN network. Electronics **10**, 864 (2021)
21. Wadatkar, P., Chaudhari, B., Zennaro, M.: Impact of interference on LoRaWAN link performance. In: Proceedings - 2019 5th International Conference on Computing, Communication Control and Automation, ICCUBEA 2019 (2019)
22. Ruotsalainen, H.: Reactive jamming detection for LoRaWAN based on meta-data differencing. In: ACM International Conference Proceeding Series (2022)
23. RN2483 LoRa Transceiver Module. http://ww1.microchip.com/downloads/en/DeviceDoc/RN2483-Low-Power-Long-Range-LoRa-Technology-Transceiver-Module-Data-Sheet-DS50002346D.pdf. Accessed 21 Jan 2023
24. ESP32 Technical Reference Manual. https://www.espressif.com/sites/default/files/documentation/esp32_technical_reference_manual_en.pdf. Accessed 20 Jan 2023

25. SX1276-7-8-9 Datasheet. https://semtech.my.salesforce.com/sfc/p/#E0000000Je lG/a/2R0000001Rbr/6EfVZUorrpoKFfvaF_Fkpgp5kzjiNyiAbqcpqh9qSjE. Accessed 20 Jan 2023
26. USRP E312 Datasheet. https://www.ettus.com/wp-content/uploads/2019/01/USRP_E312_Datasheet.pdf. Accessed 20 Jan 2023
27. Tapparel, J., Afisiadis, O., Mayoraz, P., Balatsoukas-Stimming, A., Burg, A.: An open-source LoRa physical layer prototype on GNU radio. In: 2020 IEEE 21st International Workshop on Signal Processing Advances in Wireless Communications (SPAWC) (2020)
28. Eletreby, R., Zhang, D., Kumar, S., Yagan, O.: Empowering low-power wide area networks in urban settings. In: SIGCOMM 2017 - Proceedings of the 2017 Conference of the ACM Special Interest Group on Data Communication, pp. 309–321 (2017)

People-to-Machine
or Machine-to-People (P2M) or (M2P)

What is a Good API? A Survey on the Use and Design of Application Programming Interfaces

Natalie Kiesler$^{(\boxtimes)}$ and Daniel Schiffner

DIPF Leibniz Institute for Research and Information in Education,
Frankfurt am Main, Germany
{kiesler,schiffner}@dipf.de

Abstract. In the Internet of Everything context, relevant and valuable connections between people, data, processes, and things are core elements. Machine-to-Machine (M2M) connections can be achieved, for example, by using application programming interfaces (APIs). However, investigating quality criteria of APIs has not yet gained significant traction in computing, or computing education research. In this work, we present a study of quality criteria for APIs to identify which factors developers rate as important when it comes to an API's quality. We then discuss how we can possibly quantify these factors. To achieve these goals, an online survey with experienced developers was conducted (n = 19). The results reveal that developers seem to appreciate established, stable solutions, the availability of examples, and a community. Developers also consider it important that an API can be extended, and integrated into an existing framework. However, strong trends among the criteria were not identified, as many factors play a role when choosing an API. Therefore more research is required to provide guidance to (future) software developers on how they can improve the design of their APIs.

Keywords: Internet of Everything · machine-to-machine · M2M · Application Programming Interface · API use · API design · API criteria

1 Introduction

The Internet of Everything (IoE) can be defined "as a distributed network of connections between people, smart things, processes, and data, whereas these components interact and exchange real-time data." [4] Valuable connections between these four pillars include people-to-people (P2P), machine-to-machine (M2M), and people-to-machine (P2M) systems.

To create a connection between products or services, especially in the M2M context, application programming interfaces (APIs) are the common basis for this exchange, enabling that products and services can communicate. APIs also

© ICST Institute for Computer Sciences, Social Informatics and Telecommunications Engineering 2024
Published by Springer Nature Switzerland AG 2024. All Rights Reserved
T. Pereira et al. (Eds.): IOECON 2023, LNICST 551, pp. 45–55, 2024.
https://doi.org/10.1007/978-3-031-51572-9_4

allow programmers to create new services and provide necessary insights to interact with existing methods. They can help ease a service's administration, its use, make it more flexible, and serve as a basis for innovation. Thus, APIs are a crucial technology within the context of the IoE, where connections between people, data, processes, and things are a core element.

Yet there is surprisingly little work on how to design usable APIs and how API designers may evaluate their usability prior to publishing them. When it comes to a definition of a "good" API, no clear criteria seem to exist [12]. Even though some best practice examples are identified in the literature [11, 14], and challenges developers encounter while working with an API have been investigated [9], a concrete, hands-on characterization of a high-quality API still requires research. In fact, there is little work on the design of usable APIs and how developers can evaluate their usability [3,13]. Some even resume that "Due to its nature, classification of API research is daunting for researchers" [14].

In the present work, we begin with an evaluation of good practices and how developers actually consume APIs developed by others. We, therefore, designed an online questionnaire to answer the following research question:

– RQ: *What are important factors for developers when it comes to an API's quality?*

The **goal** of this work is to identify whether and how we can classify the quality of APIs by means of quality criteria and other factors important to developers using APIs. We will then discuss how we can possibly quantify these factors. These insights, in turn, will potentially lead to better APIs and guidance for developers to increase the usability of existing and new APIs and services. The results further have implications for computing education and how to prepare software engineers for the IoE.

The structure of this paper is as follows. Related research on APIs, best practices, and challenges are presented in the following section. Section 3 outlines the research design before the results of the conducted survey are introduced in Sect. 4. Their discussion in Sect. 5 is followed by conclusions and future work.

2 Background

We reviewed several related studies and technical guidelines that define either the maturity of an API or focus on usability for developers. Looking at technical guidelines, one can find the CESSDA Technical Guidelines [1] which demand extensive resources, and thus time and effort to achieve high-quality software. For design purposes, requirement analysis is one of the key factors that is mentioned throughout the literature, as pointed out by [15]. In a technical report, Charest and Rogers [2] derive a list of methodologies when just focusing on data exchange alone. They explain the benefits and drawbacks when utilizing these methodologies as part of an API.

Meng et al. [11] use a different approach, identifying the topic from a learning perspective and how to structure documentation most effectively. They conducted two studies, one interview, and one questionnaire. They found evidence of two personas looking at APIs, who have different learning strategies. They claim that documentation is an important asset and requires more than just expertise from software developers, but also information design and communication professionals. An interesting note is that the majority of participants in the studies (106 out of 110) voted for the integration of code examples into API documentation.

Maalej and Robillard [9] evaluated the content of Java SDK and .NET API references in 2013. At this point in time, the second largest contributor was represented by information units classified as "non-information", often found in methods and fields. The authors define the so-called "non-information" as "a section of documentation containing any complete sentence or self-contained fragment of text that provides only uninformative boilerplate text" [9]. Thus, the sole documentation of all fields and methods is not improving quality. Instead, it actually hinders readability and hence can reduce the perceived quality of an API's documentation.

Ofoeda et al. [14] provide an overview of API research using a socio-technical perspective. They argue that this additional perspective is important as developers, i.e. users of an API, are the target audience. In their study, they identify a number of research topics in the context of API design, whereas API development, documentation, usage, and security are predominant. They also state that: "Nonetheless, there remains a clear gap in the adoption and use of APIs since peer-reviewed articles are lacking." [14] They conclude, among other things, that a theoretical understanding of APIs is required and further insights into APIs are needed. The authors further conclude that a poor API design and bad implementation can lead to significant challenges for companies [14].

According to Murphy et al., "prior research has shown that APIs commonly suffer from significant usability problems" and "little attention has been given to studying how APIs are designed and created in the first place" [12]. Murphy et al. further resume about best practices, such as following API design guidelines, which might be locally defined or adapted from other companies. An API should be defined by an interdisciplinary team, while a designer is responsible for taking care of all perspectives. If the goal is to create a public API, i.e. customers or users are relying on it in their own code, the burden is even higher: "To avoid "breaking changes", it is important that the API designers get core abstractions and core methods of the API correct the first time". [12] To ensure this, Murphy et al. propose getting regular feedback from API users by using Human-Computer-Interaction methods, such as user studies or personas. However, the challenge of how to generate a good and reliable design remains, as only some additional hints on how to improve the quality are provided.

In the context of computing education and research, it seems as if there is still a lack of conscientiousness for software and its contribution to the epistemological process in general [8]. The development of tools as a research area is described as challenging "both for designing and reporting research" [10]. However, we need to invest more effort into the investigation and reporting of software (including, e.g., APIs) as part of the research process [5,6]. This is especially true in the IoE context, where improving the quality of an API may have a tremendous impact on future services, data, things, and eventually people [7].

3   Research Design

The present work aims at the identification of factors developers rate as important when it comes to the quality of APIs. To achieve this and better understand the developer's perspective, the authors conducted an online survey focusing on the use of APIs. It contained open and closed questions, clustered within three sections:

1. General questions and prior experience (3 open and 6 closed questions)
2. Criteria of good APIs (2 closed questions)
3. Criteria for using an API (5 open 2 and closed questions)

The full list of questions is summarized in the Appendix. Answering all questions was expected to last between 15 and 20 min. Participation in the survey was voluntary. Anyone could withdraw from the participation at any time without giving any reasons and without experiencing any disadvantages. No personal information was collected, and the data cannot be attributed to an individual. Study participants further received information on their legal rights granted by the General Data Protection Regulation. Moreover, the study was approved by the ethics board of the authors' institution.

The survey was distributed among teams containing software developers and computing researchers at several German research institutes within the Leibniz community via e-mail and internal chats. Due to this interdisciplinary, international work environment with English as *lingua franca*, the survey was made available in both German and English. It was online for four weeks, with one reminder message being sent to the addressed target audience after two weeks.

4   Results

In this section, we summarize the results beginning with the general questions and prior experience (see Appendix, Section I) to characterize the sample. The main sections (II and III) of the survey are summarized in alignment with the research question stated before. We thus point out important API characteristics from the developer's perspective.

4.1   Characteristics of the Sample

In total, 19 responses have been collected that almost completely answered the questionnaire. The majority of the 19 respondents is either a software developer (n = 8), a researcher in the context of computer science (n = 8), or employed in a coordinating or leading position (n = 3). Most respondents are experienced programmers, with 12 of them having more than 10 years of programming experience, two have 6 to 10 years of experience, four have 3 to 5 years of experience, and one person has 0 to 2 years of experience.

When asked about their prior experience in using APIs in years, seven persons replied as having more than 5 years, four have 4 to 5 years, four others have 2 to 3 years, and yet another four have 0 to 1 year of experience. We also gathered details from respondents on previous experience with using APIs from other developers. Five persons have used more than 10, seven have used 5 to 10, and the remaining seven have used 1 to 5 APIs from other developers. Hence, we can conclude all respondents have experience with using APIs.

For the question of how they learned using APIs, candidates could select multiple answers. Here, 16 of 19 respondents stated that they developed their competencies related to APIs via informal education (e.g., own research, literature, etc.). As this was a multiple choice question, 11 replies indicate it was due to professional practice, eight due to higher education, and seven due to further training (on-the-job). Three responses provided vocational training as educational background.

The survey further asked for the types of APIs respondents are using. In this multiple-choice question, open/public APIs were selected 16 times, and internal APIs 13 times. Both, external APIs and authentification APIs were each selected by 12 respondents. When asked for the context of their API use, a variety of topics was provided, such as education ($n = 7$), research ($n = 5$), Natural Language Processing ($n = 5$), research data center ($n = 4$), repositories ($n = 3$), library services ($n = 2$), as well as information gathering and management ($n = 2$). Other contexts mentioned by the participants were social media ($n = 1$), knowledge graphs ($n = 1$), identity management ($n = 1$), tools ($n = 1$), and infrastructure in general ($n = 1$).

We further asked for the programming language preferably used for working with APIs (as an open question), and received the following replies: Python ($n = 10$), Java ($n = 7$), Javascript ($n = 6$), C# ($n = 2$), as well as PHP ($n = 1$) and Perl ($n = 1$). Interestingly, data formats (JSON, $n = 1$, and XML, $n = 1$) were among the replies. Respondents mostly use APIs for the backend ($n = 17$), but also for frontend development ($n = 13$), whereas 11 persons use APIs for both areas.

4.2 Important Factors for Developers

The second and third section of the survey (see Appendix) focused on crucial API criteria from a developer's perspective. The responses will be presented next to answer the research question.

As part of that, survey participants were asked to rate the importance of several API features, assuming they are having a choice of which API to use. We then offered five answer pairs on a bipolar, seven-point Likert scale. The five answer pairs containing opposites comprise:

(a) Stability vs. Up-to-dateness
(b) Support offers vs. Extendability
(c) Integration in an existing framework vs. Required duration for getting started
(d) Documentation vs. Focus on solutions
(e) Established Solution vs. Innovative solution

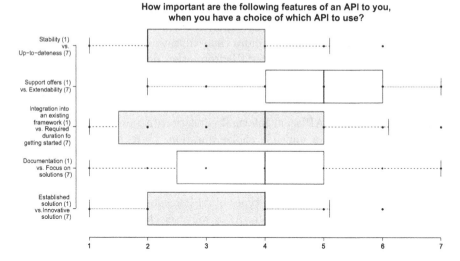

Fig. 1. Box plot of the responses to the question on feature preferences of APIs (n = 19).

The responses to these five answer pairs are summarized in Fig. 1. They indicate a median of 2 leaning towards the stability of an API (Mean 2,7 and SD 1,4) as an important feature. The surveyed developers favored the extendability of an API over available support offers (Mean 4,8 and SD 1,6). The integration into an existing framework seems more important than the required duration it takes to get started (Mean 3,4 and SD 1,9). The median, however, is 4. The same median applies to the remaining two answer pairs (d) and (e). Rating the importance of available documentation versus a focus on solutions also resulted in a mean of 4, and a standard deviation of 1,8 indicating that developers are undecided. For the last answer pair, the mean is 3,2 (SD 1,5), so developers seem to favor established solutions somewhat more than innovative ones.

The next question focused on important factors when actually using an API. Figure 2 represents how the respondents rated eight factors on a five-point unipolar Likert scale ranging from *absolutely essential* to *not important at all*. In addition, *I can't say* was offered as an answering option. All of the 19 surveyed persons replied to the question. The highest level of agreement (i.e., the addition of the ratings as *absolutely essential* and *very important*) were found related to the existence of examples of the API's use (n = 16), and a rigorous naming of functions, variables, and methods (n = 16). Similarly, an existing community (e.g., on GitHub, Stack Overflow, etc.) is rated as absolutely essential or very important by 14 respondents. The effort required for familiarizing one's self with how the API actually works (n = 12), as well as the sound embedding in the debugging process (n = 10) further play a crucial role for many API users. Nonetheless, it seems as if all of the surveyed factors do play a role when using an API, but with slightly varying weight.

How important are the following factors when using an API?

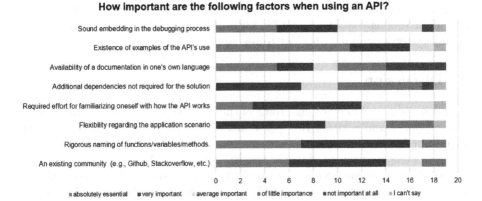

Fig. 2. Responses to the question on important features when using an API (n = 19).

Asking the developers about the importance of flexibility that usually comes with REST APIs, 14 participants answered that it is one of their driving factors to select them. Only four participants stated otherwise, while one did not answer the question. When explaining their selection, the developers stated in the negative case that usually no other option would be available, or that flexibility can cause security issues.

We further asked for the developers' own criteria as an open question. It contains, among other aspects, "ease of use", documentation, dependencies, or time needed for integration as important criteria. One developer expressed it in a very philosophical manner:

> In the best case, the API integrates well into the framework and stands on the shoulders of the giant instead of fighting it.

When we asked whether or not the developers have always adhered to their own criteria, the answers were almost evenly distributed between adhering to their rules (n = 9) and breaking them (n = 7).

The open question on important factors for the integration of APIs made the surveyed developers more conservative. Several participants responded with answers favoring a clear structure and modularization. However, no clear trend can be identified and seven persons did not even answer this question.

The final question set focused on the challenges when implementing APIs and how to overcome them. Among bad documentation (n = 6), and lack of availability if provided by a third party (n = 3), there were concerns regarding long-term maintenance and compatibility (n = 3). Seven participants did not answer the question. When asked how to overcome these issues, some participants (n = 8) responded with common terms among *Developer User Experience*, such as "easy to learn", "clear contracts" or "graceful version transition". One answer actually included the active use of test cases to learn the API:

> [...], I learn by examining the test cases how to utilize the API.

Some respondents were stating that the bigger picture needs to be involved and automatic tooling could help simplify some of the tasks. One participant fell out of this pattern, by mandating not to use third-party APIs.

5   Discussion

In this section, we briefly discuss some of the most interesting aspects of the survey responses, while considering possibilities to quantify the factors considered important by the developers.

One of the most repeated inputs was the community-building aspect. Having an (a)synchronous method for communication was considered the most helpful resource when using an API. Similarly, developers repeatedly referred to documentation, but well beyond the classical text document. Short examples on how to use the API together with concise code documentation were considered to be most helpful. One participant also stated that they like to utilize test cases to better understand an API. This underlines that the examples do not need to be artificial, but can utilize existing methods for code quality.

In the bipolar Likert scale, we asked for different trade-offs. Stability, extendability, and established solutions were rated as being more important. Given their long experience in programming, we assume the developers had their fair share of breaking APIs and incompatibilities. Support for them is not the key factor when selecting an API in the first place. This is also reflected in the answer to innovative solutions, which tend to be in a state of flux and thus change more often. The other two dimensions, however, have not been as clear. Integration was considered to be more relevant than the duration it takes to get started. This can be interpreted as the reuse of code and patterns being very important, especially in long-term maintenance projects. Documentation, on the other hand, was not a clear favorite, mainly due to the fact that the other dimension might not be as contradictory as initially thought. Good documentation might focus on the solution of an actual problem and hence contribute to the solution.

While not stated explicitly, a lot of the answers are aimed at the Developer User Experience (DevUX). "Ease of use", "easy to learn" or "community" are elements supporting a better DevUX. As numerous APIs exist, sole functionality is not a deciding factor anymore. Developers tend to favor other factors over pure innovation or problem-solving. These factors should also be taken into account when "designing" an API.

Quantifying the results factors remains somewhat challenging. Measuring when an API is "easy to use" certainly requires more research before this factor can be evaluated. Criteria where a quantification seems reasonable comprise:

- the duration of time required for developers to familiarize themselves with the API,
- the availability of examples, and use cases,
- the API's complexity,
- the extent to which an API's documentation contains methods which are explained with reference to their objective,

- the deliverable of an API,
- an API's availability,
- an API's security.

Some of these criteria have also been reported in prior work. Maalej and Robillard [9] have already criticized the level of "non-information" within API documentation. Therefore, explaining an API's method with regard to its objective seems to be a more promising quality criterion. Murphy et al. [12] have also discussed the impact of APIs on security. It thus seems reasonable to include this aspect as a quality criterion.

Limitations of the present work concern the small sample size. With 19 respondents from several German research institutes, the survey is limited to one country and the context of educational technology, and infrastructure research. Moreover, the nature of the survey was somewhat exploratory due to the lack of a great body of prior research. Hence, it is not yet possible to define strict, or clear-cut criteria for APIs.

6   Conclusion and Future Work

Application Programming Interfaces (APIs) are crucial to achieve machine-to-machine connections within the Internet of Everything. In this study, we explored and identified important criteria for developers when using APIs, and how we can possibly quantify them. The starting point of this research was the lack of both research and common approaches toward a good API's design, usability, or other criteria. We, therefore, conducted a study with software developers and computing researchers who have experience in using APIs. The results of the online survey revealed that developers value stable, established solutions with rigorous naming and a community or examples they can relate to when making the effort to familiarize themselves with the API. Similarly, the possibility to extend an API, and integrate it into an existing framework is appreciated, whereas the required effort itself plays an important role. In summary, all of the surveyed factors do play a role when using an API, while their degree of importance and related challenges slightly vary. Moreover, it is still challenging to quantify some of the criteria indicating an API's quality, and increasing its use by others. Nonetheless, the gathered insights can be a reference for educating future software engineers, who will likely design services and products for or in the context of the IoE.

As the results of this work have implications for research, practice, and educators, there are several pathways for future work. One of them is to continue our efforts to identify and quantify the quality criteria of APIs and conduct a follow-up study with developers. Another approach is to expand the scope of the survey to other institutions and industry or to qualitatively address the developer's perspective. The latter could lead to an increased understanding of the conditions for certain preferences and tendencies. Yet another future research approach is to analyze popular, publicly available APIs with regard to the criteria investigated in this study.

Appendix

Survey Questions

Section I - General Questions and Prior Experience

1. Current job title
2. Your programming experience in years
3. Your experience in using APIs in years
4. How many APIs from other developers have you used so far?
5. How did you develop your competencies related to APIs?
6. Which types of APIs are you using?
7. In which context are you using APIs (e.g., education, research data center, natural language processing, etc.)?
8. Which programming language(s) do you prefer to use for working with an API?
9. For which interfaces do you use APIs?

Section II - Criteria of Good APIs

1. Assume there are several APIs available to choose from. How important are the following features of an API to you, when you have a choice of which API to use?
2. How important are the following factors when using an API?

Section III - Criteria for Using an API

1. Open API architectures (such as REST) offer creative freedom in API design. Is this flexibility a factor that drives you to use them?
2. Please explain your selection regarding flexibility as a factor (see previous question).
3. Which criteria do you use to evaluate the complexity of integrating a new API into an existing system/framework?
4. Have you ever encountered cases where the criteria you mentioned regarding the complexity of an API did not play a role in your choice?
5. What factors in your system architecture make it easier for you to integrate existing APIs?
6. Which challenges (due to the API and the system) have you already experienced when integrating third-party APIs?
7. Do you have ideas on how to overcome these challenges?

References

1. CESSDA Technical Guidelines (2023). https://docs.tech.cessda.eu/
2. Charest, G., Rogers, M.: Data exchange mechanisms and considerations. https://enterprisearchitecture.harvard.edu/data-exchange-mechanisms

3. Horvath, A., Nagy, M., Voichick, F., Kery, M.B., Myers, B.A.: Methods for investigating mental models for learners of APIs. In: Extended Abstracts of the 2019 CHI Conference on Human Factors in Computing Systems, CHI EA 2019, pp. 1–6. ACM, New York (2019). https://doi.org/10.1145/3290607.3312897

4. Kiesler, N., Impagliazzo, J.: Perspectives on the internet of everything. In: Pereira, T., Impagliazzo, J., Santos, H. (eds.) IoECon 2022. LNICST, vol. 458, pp. 3–17. Springer, Cham (2023). https://doi.org/10.1007/978-3-031-25222-8_1

5. Kiesler, N., Schiffner, D.: On the lack of recognition of software artifacts and IT infrastructure in educational technology research. In: Henning, P.A., Striewe, M., Wölfel, M. (eds.) 20. Fachtagung Bildungstechnologien (DELFI), pp. 201–206. Gesellschaft für Informatik e.V., Bonn (2022). https://doi.org/10.18420/delfi2022-034

6. Kiesler, N., Schiffner, D.: Why we need open data in computer science education research. In: Proceedings of the 2023 Conference on Innovation and Technology in Computer Science Education, ITiCSE 2023, vol. 1. Association for Computing Machinery, New York (2023). https://doi.org/10.1145/3587102.3588860

7. Kiesler, N., Thorbrügge, C.: Socially responsible programming in computing education and expectations in the profession. In: Proceedings of the 2023 Conference on Innovation and Technology in Computer Science Education, ITiCSE 2023, vol. 1, pp. 443–449. Association for Computing Machinery, New York (2023). https://doi.org/10.1145/3587102.3588839

8. Kinnunen, P., Meisalo, V., Malmi, L.: Have we missed something? Identifying missing types of research in computing education. In: Proceedings of the Sixth International Workshop on Computing Education Research, ICER 2010, pp. 13–22. ACM, New York (2010). https://doi.org/10.1145/1839594.1839598

9. Maalej, W., Robillard, M.: Patterns of knowledge in API reference documentation. IEEE Trans. Softw. Eng. **39**, 1264–1282 (2013). https://doi.org/10.1109/TSE.2013.12

10. Malmi, L.: Tools research-what is it? ACM Inroads **5**(3), 34–35 (2014). https://doi.org/10.1145/2655759.2655768

11. Meng, M., Steinhardt, S., Schubert, A.: Application programming interface documentation: what do software developers want? J. Tech. Writ. Commun. **48**(3), 295–330 (2018). https://doi.org/10.1177/0047281617721853

12. Murphy, L., Kery, M.B., Alliyu, O., Macvean, A., Myers, B.A.: API designers in the field: design practices and challenges for creating usable APIs. In: 2018 IEEE Symposium on Visual Languages and Human-Centric Computing (VL/HCC), pp. 249–258 (2018). https://doi.org/10.1109/VLHCC.2018.8506523

13. Myers, B.A., Stylos, J.: Improving API usability. Commun. ACM **59**(6), 62–69 (2016). https://doi.org/10.1145/2896587

14. Ofoeda, J., Boateng, R., Effah, J.: Application programming interface (API) research: a review of the past to inform the future. Int. J. Enterp. Inf. Syst. (IJEIS) **15**(3), 76–95 (2019)

15. Zowghi, D., Coulin, C.: Requirements elicitation: a survey of techniques, approaches, and tools. In: Aurum, A., Wohlin, C. (eds.) Engineering and Managing Software Requirements, pp. 19–46. Springer, Heidelberg (2005). https://doi.org/10.1007/3-540-28244-0_2

Machine Learning for Insurance Fraud Detection

Maria Chousa Santos[1]([✉]), Teresa Pereira[2], Isabel Mendes[3],
and António Amaral[4]

[1] University of Minho, Braga, Portugal
a89166@alunos.uminho.pt
[2] School of Engineering (DIS), University of Minho, Guimarães, Portugal
[3] School of Technology and Management (ESTGA), University of Aveiro, Águeda,
Portugal
[4] Polytechnic of Porto - School of Engineering (ISEP), Porto, Portugal

Abstract. Fraudulent activities are a complex problem, and still evolve in a continual basis in all company sectors. These activities are considered as one of the major difficulties the insurance companies have to deal with on a daily basis. Thus, insurers are looking for ways to effectively manage, control, and mitigate fraud. In addition, improving profits by minimizing fraud is the main goal. The exponential amount of information collected, and the technology evolvement has been a strategy to address frauds. The Internet of Everything enables organizations to access diverse information's resources through the interconnection of people-to-machines, which involves machines, data and people, contributing to increase their knowledge and intelligence. In the world of technology, Machine Learning has been widely implemented in multiple contexts. The insurers companies start using Machine Learning to support the detection of fraudulent complaints through the application of algorithms aimed to find patterns in a database, which are hidden through a large amount of data. This paper intends to present the use of Machine Learning technology to support the insurers companies to detect fraudulent activities and further analyze the impacts of technology in people and thus enable to achieve a more rapid and accurate information.

Keywords: Insurance · Fraud · Machine Learning-IoE · Artificial Intelligence

1 Introduction

The core of a company's mission revolves around its people, as they are essential to its growth. The Internet of Everything (IoE) refers to the interconnectedness of people, processes, data, and things, which enabling real-time data extraction and analysis, with a focus on automating processes for the benefit of individuals and organizations. Previously separate entities are now connected to the internet,

T. Pereira et al. (Eds.): IOECON 2023, LNICST 551, pp. 56–65, 2024.
https://doi.org/10.1007/978-3-031-51572-9_5

including machine-to-machine (M2M), person-to-machine (P2M), and person-to-person (P2P) systems. The convergence of these elements through the IoE allows businesses to leverage their benefits and accomplish their objectives [17].

Technology is clearly an important factor in the IoE. Langley et al. [13] divide the IoE into 4 areas:

- IoT - is a subset of IoE, which connects things to provide new possibilities for enhancing the level of intelligence of things;
- Data - is considered the key, enabling technological development, driving the growth of smart things;
- Artificial Intelligence - where "intelligent" things are understood as objects that are sensing, reasoning and performing actions based on input data to achieve a certain predefined goal;
- Semantic Interoperability - the ability of heterogeneous devices to understand each other.

Insurers companies encounter a significant challenge in identifying and detecting fraud committed by policyholders. Given the severity of this issue and the substantial financial losses it can incur for insurers, this work aims to present a solution to mitigate or minimize the impact of fraud in these organizations.

The aim of this study is to explore a solution that can aid in identifying fraudulent claims, thereby minimizing the harm caused to organizations. Additionally, the study presented seeks to address the main research question: how do models inherent to Machine Learning assist and enhance fraud detection measures in insurance companies?

This paper is organized as follows: Sect. 2 provides an overview of the insurance industry, with a specific focus on auto insurance. This section will also provide information on fraud and its detection; Sect. 3 deepens the study in a more specific manner, exploring the use of Artificial Intelligence and Machine Learning technologies in detecting fraud, and presenting possible solutions; lastly, in Sects. 4 and 5 are presented conclusions and outlines future work, respectively.

2   Insurance Business Area Overview and Fraud

In 2020, the insurance penetration rate in OECD (Organization for Economic Co-operation and Development) countries was 9.4%. This suggests that the insurance industry plays a significant role as a key component of the global economy [12]. Why is insurance so important? Insurance plays a critical role in a company's growth by protecting its financial well-being. Insurance companies provide information about potential risks and the likelihood of loss, thereby minimizing investment risk. As a result, insurers can motivate companies to take a long-term view and increase their risk tolerance. Insurance companies also make a significant contribution to the growth of the capital market in the global economy by managing substantial assets, enabling them to mobilize national savings and bridge the investment gap in emerging markets [7].

2.1 Fraud

Fraudulent activities, such as malicious acts, pose different financial and legal problems in different markets. Within the insurance industry, a significant number of fraud cases are identified each year when, according to the report on insurance fraud presented by FRISS in 2022, 18 % of claims in 2020 were fraudulent and in 2021 this figure rose to 20 % [8], and it is estimated that fraudulent claims account for 10 % of claims costs in Europe [19].

A study has identified a generic fraud control model that an insurer goes through when it receives a new claim, as shown in Fig. 1. This model consists of three distinct phases. The first phase, focuses on determining the nature of the complaint. It can be resolved quickly and at minimal costs if it is determined to be non-suspicious.

However, if the complaint is considered suspicious, it requires a human investigation, resulting in higher costs and resource utilization.

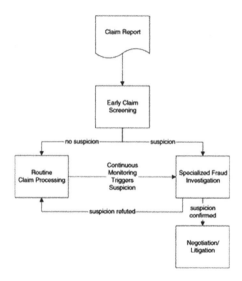

Fig. 1. Fraud control model, source [21]

The second phase, known as the investigation, involves the use of specialized investigators who conduct a rigorous and meticulous investigation to uncover the true nature of the complaint, whether it is fraudulent or not. Finally, in the last phase, the fraudulent claim is dealt with either through negotiation or litigation [21].

The costs associated with investigating and resolving fraudulent claims can be a significant financial burden for insurers, which ultimately impacts honest customers through higher premiums. Furthermore, such fraudulent activities create intense competitive pressure within the insurance market, compelling insurers to enhance the attractiveness of their products to customers [9].

While investigating suspicious claims can be a valuable exercise, it is important to note that it comes with an additional cost to the insurer. The costs of investigating fraudulent claims often exceeds the amount recovered, resulting in financial loss to the insurer. Consequently, the costs of fraudulent claims affects the profitability of the insurer and can lead to higher premiums for honest customers.

2.2 Car Insurance

Regarding the products that insurers provide is auto insurance, which has been found to be significantly impacted by fraudulent activity, according to several research studies [20]. Car insurance is mandatory in the European Union, and covers bodily injury and property damage incurred by third parties and passengers. When it comes to this type of insurance, there are many factors that affect customers and their insurance premiums. Some of these factors include the driver's experience, age, and vehicle specifications, as well as the expected repair costs in the event of an accident [4].

2.3 Fraud Detection

Although there are several approaches to mitigating fraud in the insurance industry. There is no definitive solution that is both completely effective and efficient. One possible measure is the sharing of relevant information among insurers to facilitate the detection of potential fraud. Border cooperation, the creation of a dedicated fraud investigation team, partnerships with law enforcement agencies in different countries, and training for insurers' employees can also help in reducing fraudulent activity [19].

The ways in which fraud is reduced and detected have been evolving with the emergence of new technology. Increasingly, researchers are exploring potential solutions that involve Machine Learning and Artificial Intelligence to develop predictive techniques that can improve the detection of fraudulent activity. The following section, introduces Artificial Intelligence approaches to reducing fraud.

3 Artificial Intelligence Approach in Insurance Fraud Detection

As technology evolves, insurances exploit the potential of those technologies developing applications to detect and mitigate fraud. Increasingly, potential solutions using Machine Learning and Artificial Intelligence are being explored to implement predictive fraud detection techniques.

Artificial Intelligence and Machine Learning can be a valuable starting point to address part of this problem: Artificial Intelligence automatically learns from data, enabling to make predictions and estimate actions. Additionally, Machine Learning techniques can further extend the potential for prediction-making by uncovering implicit or concealed correlations [6].

Benedek and László [4] suggested using data mining algorithms to address fraud detection. These are designed to search for patterns in a database that may be difficult to identify due to the large amount of data involved. This study aimed to determine the most effective of three methods: Decision Tree, Neural Networks, and Naive Bayes. The researchers identified key factors in analyzing the data, including vehicle make, accident location, policyholder age and marital status, policy type, and the vehicle category and price. After analysing the data, the researchers concluded that the Decision Tree algorithm outperformed the other methods and was therefore the best choice.

Alternatively, some studies approach fraud detection as a classification issue and propose methods such as Logistic Regression, Decision Tree, K-Nearest Neighbor, Bayesian Neural Networks, among others [9]. While there are numerous studies detailing strategies to reduce fraudulent activity, most of them rely on the implementation of Machine Learning techniques and their corresponding algorithms.

3.1 Machine Learning

Machine Learning is a type of Artificial Intelligence that enables machines to effectively interpret data through data learning. It uses mathematical models called algorithms to collect and analyze data to make a final decision that matches the user's request. This technology has the ability to perform tasks automatically and to learn from the data that is provided to it [15].

Machine Learning offers several types of analysis, two of which are classification and regression analysis. Classification analysis uses algorithms to make decisions or predict behavior, making it relevant to fraud detection. Regression analysis, on the other hand, attempts to predict the outcome of a continuous variable based on one or more values. These two analyses differ in their predictive content, with classification predicting variables from different classes and regression providing continuous prediction. Since the goal of this study is to identify suspected fraudulent claims, classification analysis is the most appropriate. Using algorithms such as the Decision Tree, Naive Bayes and other classification algorithms, suspicious requests are flagged based on the results of this analysis, since this type of algorithm tries to predict a certain behavior using variables from different classes.

3.2 Technologies Solutions

Today, there are solutions that can identify cases of fraud. FRISS is as an example of an organization that provides such solutions. Among the products offered, by this organization is one dedicated to detecting fraudulent activity. This specific product uses Artificial Intelligence and transparent predictive models to prevent fraud in real-time. This creates a scenario where the insurer can avoid paying the customer's claim. [10]. SAS provides cutting-edge technologies powered by Artificial Intelligence that enable faster, more efficient analysis. Among the software solutions that SAS offers, it focus on fraud detection and prevention.

SAS Detection and Investigation for Insurance is an advanced software program designed to identify, prevent and monitor fraudulent behavior associated with insurance claims. This software leverages a range of analytical techniques and Artificial Intelligence technologies, such as Machine Learning and deep learning, to improve its detection capabilities. [18].

SHIFT is a company that provides decision-making solutions based on Artificial Intelligence. The company is focused on providing solutions that enable insurance companies to automate and streamline their decision-making processes, resulting to increased operational efficiency and reduced costs. One of the many solutions provided by SHIFT is the Shift Claims Fraud Detection tool. This tool is capable of detecting fraud in claims in real-time and provides all the relevant information about the claim, along with a detailed explanation of the conclusion reached [11].

Linkurious is a company that specializes in graph intelligence solutions that help to easily connect complex data to enable faster more informed business decisions. Its anti-fraud solution combines Machine Learning with graph analytic to create a network of customers and their connections in a matter of seconds. By doing so, it provides the ability to see the full context of a customer or suspicious claim, filter the data, explore other relationships, and ultimately dismantle fraud networks [14].

The Table 1 provides a clearer overview of the characteristics of the solutions offered by the companies.

Table 1. Solution's Comparison.

	FRISS	SAS	Shift	Linkurious
Velocity of investigations	–	–	3x faster	Increase up to 10x
Number of insurers and countries involved	Over 200 insurers in more than 40 countries	Almost 150 countries	More than 25 countries	2000 companies
Implementation Time	4 months	–	4 months	–
Number of risk assessments per year	26 million	–	Hundreds of millions	–
Reduce case alert volume	–	40 %	–	–
Expose fraud	–	35 %	–	Up to 20 %

The data presented in the table indicates that the average implementation time for each solution is four months, a reasonable and typical duration that can yield significant benefits to the implementing company. The table shows several metrics that support the argument, such as the millions of annual assessments, the reduction in alert cases, and the expedited investigations. These indicators ultimately lead to the primary issue addressed in the table, which is the mitigation of fraud exposure. Typically, increasing the speed of investigations allows companies to handle cases more efficiently, resulting in greater customer satisfaction with the promptness of the process. In addition, as noted above, minimizing the risk of fraud provides benefits to organizations, such as reduced costs and improved financial stability.

4   Adapting Data and Using Machine Learning

Analyzing the insurance company's data is a crucial step in applying Machine Learning models. Studying the variables individually, taking into account the description of each column, the values it aggregates, the type of data, in order to help clean the data and make any necessary changes, are some steps required to clean the data. Once the data has been cleaned and the necessary changes have been made, the relationships between the various attributes are assessed using a correlation matrix, i.e., Pearson Correlation, Spearman, Kendall, among others. These matrix's have different objectives, Pearson's correlation focuses on the strength of the linear relationship between two vectors of data, while Spearman's correlation only describes the monotonic degree [22]. Kendall's correlation assesses the similarity between two sets of classifications on the same data [1]. Among these correlations, the one that is most appropriate and the one that will be applied is Pearson's correlation, since it obtains linear correlations of quantitative variables.

The Pearson correlation matrix provides values between 0 and 1 (absolute) where the higher the value, the greater the relationship between the attributes, known as coefficients. Correlation coefficients are generally used as a first tool to quantify, visualize and interpret relationships between different attributes. Once the correlations have been assessed, it is possible to differentiate between certain attributes and remove those with a very weak correlation, in order to obtain a dataset with a set of specific attributes.

Azure offers various services and tools for applying DevOps practices that focus on automating and optimizing processes using this technology, including continuous integration and continuous delivery (CI/CD) [5]. Azure Pipelines is one example. This allows CI/CD to be implemented to create, test and deploy continuously, on any platform and in any cloud [2]. Azure currently offers the ability to study the best Machine Learning model for a given data set and train it continuously. In this way, any insurance company can apply Machine Learning models to its data without requiring much effort or knowledge on the subject. Despite this Azure offering, each insurance company also has the opportunity to choose its own model and apply it.

However, it is necessary to mention the need to carry out tests in order to detect flaws and possible improvements, where the effectiveness of a Machine Learning model in identifying fraudulent cases as correct or incorrect can be related to various causes, including: the quality of the data, limitations of the algorithm and also the complexity of the problem.

5   Conclusion and Future Work

In conclusion, the impact of fraudulent claims on the insurance market cannot be overstated, as it can destabilize economies and affect people's cost of living [3]. These consequences highlight the critical need for organizations to invest in advanced technologies to prevent fraud and protect their reputations and financial stability, since traditional methods such as hiring companies focused on assessing claims can be rather time-consuming and may not even result in a reliable response. In this context, methods involving Machine Learning are increasingly considered the best alternative, as they allow insurers to analyze the relationships between various data automatically, leading to a shortening of investigation time.

Artificial Intelligence and Machine Learning, in particular, offer promising solutions to address this issue. The potential for these technologies to transform the insurance industry was recognized by Forbes Magazine, which named Artificial Intelligence as one of the top technology trends for 2022 [16]. As Artificial Intelligence continues to advance, it is likely to become an increasingly important investment for businesses to ensure their continued success.

With this in mind, Machine Learning is poised to become a prudent investment for companies in the near future, especially in the area of fraud detection. It is important the use of classification algorithms, such as Decision Tree, Bayer Naive and Neural Net to speed up fraud investigations and identify larger fraud schemes. These algorithms have shown promising results in generating positive financial outcomes for both companies and their customers.

It's also important to focus on some future work, to obtain some results based on the research presented in this paper. Is intended to put the analysis into practice by using a dataset related to auto insurance fraud. Then apply Machine Learning models, such as Decision Tree, Bayesian Classifiers, and Neural Networks. These models are well suited for pattern recognition in complex datasets and are effective in fraud detection.

However, the development of an application that can efficiently and effectively detect fraud claims using the Machine Learning is expected. Such an application would be a valuable tool for insurance companies, allowing them to detect and prevent fraud, potentially saving them millions of dollars.

Overall, companies must remain vigilant and stay aligned with the of technological advancements in order to protect themselves from fraudulent activities. By investing in emerging technologies, such as Artificial Intelligence and Machine Learning, companies can identify patterns in large data sets that are usually difficult to detect, be more efficient, provide a faster response, safeguard their reputation, protect their customers and above all preventing fraud and maintain their financial stability in the market.

References

1. Abdi, H.: The kendall rank correlation coefficient (2007)
2. Azure Pipelines (2023). https://azure.microsoft.com/en-us/products/devops/pipe lines. Accessed 19 June 2023
3. Benedek, B., Ciumas, C., Nagy, B.Z.: Automobile insurance fraud detection in the age of big data - a systematic and comprehensive literature review. J. Finan. Regul. Compliance **30**(4), 503–523 (2022). ISSN 1358–1988. https:// doi.org/10.1108/JFRC-11-2021-0102. https://www.emerald.com/insight/content/ doi/10.1108/JFRC-11-2021-0102/full/html
4. Benedek, B., László, E.: Identifying key fraud indicators in the automobile insurance industry using SQL server analysis services. Studia Universitatis Babes-Bolyai Oeconomica **64**(2), 53–71 (2019). ISSN 2065–9644. https://doi.org/ 10.2478/subboec-2019-0009. https://www.sciendo.com/article/10.2478/subboec-2019-0009
5. DevOps (2023). https://azure.microsoft.com/pt-pt/resources/cloud-computing-di ctionary/what-is-devops. Accessed 19 June 2023
6. Eckert, C., Neunsinger, C., Osterrieder, K.: Managing customer satisfaction: digital applications for insurance companies. Geneva Pap. Risk Insur. - Issues Pract. **47**(3):569–602 (2022). ISSN 1468–0440. https://doi.org/10.1057/s41288-021-00257-z
7. Baur, E., Birkmaier, U., Rüstmann, M: The economic importance of insurance in Central and Eastern Europe and the impact of globalisation and e-business (2021)
8. FRISS - Insurance fraud report 2022 (2023). https://www.friss.com/insight/ insurance-fraud-report-2022/. Accessed 20 Jan 2023
9. Galeotti, M., Rabitti, G., Vannucci, E.: An evolutionary approach to fraud management. Eur. J. Oper. Res. **284**(3), 1167–1177 (2020). ISSN 03772217. https://doi.org/10.1016/j.ejor.2020.01.017. https://linkinghub.elsevier. com/retrieve/pii/S0377221720300382
10. Home. FRISS (2023). https://www.friss.com/. Accessed 23 Jan 2023
11. Home (2023). https://www.shift-technology.com/?hsLang=en. Accessed 24 Jan 2023
12. Insurance indicators : Penetration. https://stats.oecd.org/Index.aspx?QueryId= 25444. Accessed 20 Jan 2023
13. Langley, D.J., et al.: The internet of everything: smart things and their impact on business models. J. Bus. Res. 122, 853–863 (2021). ISSN 01482963. https://doi.org/10.1016/j.jbusres.2019.12.035. https://linkinghub.elsevier.com/ret rieve/pii/S014829631930801X
14. Linkurious — graph intelligence solutions for the enterprise — let us light the way in your connected data (2023). https://linkurious.com/. Accessed 30 Jan 2023
15. Mahesh, B.: Machine learning algorithms -a review. https://doi.org/10.21275/ ART20203995
16. Marr, B.: The 5 biggest technology trends in 2022. Forbes. Section: Enterprise Tech. (2021). https://www.forbes.com/sites/bernardmarr/2021/09/27/the-5-biggest-technology-trends-in-2022/ (visited on 01/25/2023)
17. Miraz, M.H., et al.: A review on internet of things (IoT), internet of everything (IoE) and internet of Nano things (IoNT). In: 2015 Internet Technologies and Applications (ITA), pp. 219–224 (2015). https://doi.org/10.1109/ITechA.2015. 7317398

18. SAS: analytics, artificial intelligence and data management (2023). https://www.sas.com/pt_pt/home.html. Accessed 24 Jan 2023
19. The impact of insurance fraud (2013)
20. Viaene, S., Dedene, G.: Insurance fraud: issues and challenges. Geneva Pap. Risk Insur. - Issues Pract. **29**(2), 313–333 (2019). ISSN 1018–5895, 1468–0440. https://doi.org/10.1111/j.1468-0440.2004.00290.x. http://link.springer.com/10.1111/j.1468-0440.2004.00290.x. Accessed 20 Jan 2023
21. Viaene, S., Van Gheel, D., Ayuso, M., Guillén, M.: Cost-sensitive design of claim fraud screens. In: Perner, P. (ed.) ICDM 2004. LNCS (LNAI), vol. 3275, pp. 78–87. Springer, Heidelberg (2004). https://doi.org/10.1007/978-3-540-30185-1_9
22. De Winter, J.C., Gosling, S.D., Potter, J.: Comparing the pearson and spearman correlation coefficients across distributions and sample sizes: a tutorial using simulations and empirical data. Psychol. Methods **21**(3), 273–290 (2016). ISSN 1939–1463, 1082–989X. https://doi.org/10.1037/met0000079. http://doi.apa.org/getdoi.cfm?doi=10.1037/met0000079. Accessed 19 June 2023

A Simple Distributed Approach for Running Machine Learning Based Simulations in Intrusion Detection Systems

Rui Fernandes[1] and Nuno Lopes[2,3]

[1] School of Technology, IPCA, Barcelos, Portugal
a17618@alunos.ipca.pt
[2] 2AI - School of Technology, IPCA, Barcelos, Portugal
nlopes@ipca.pt
[3] LASI - Associate Laboratory of Intelligent Systems, Guimarães, Portugal

Abstract. Intrusion Detection Systems (IDS) that use Machine Learning (ML) are a must-have for success protection when thinking of network traffic. Classification algorithms within Machine Learning have already proved their value in this research field and they are already being used in real scenarios as a service.

However, analysing large quantities of data, with possibly multiple distinct algorithms takes a considerable amount of computing and time resources on the training phase that are required to decide which is the most efficient classification model. We propose the use of a distributed computing platform, using the Ray Python Library, to deploy a simple parallel execution of ML training algorithms with minimal source code change. We use the well-known CICIDS 2017 dataset to evaluate an ML based IDS as the testing case.

The results show that the Ray library is a simple and direct approach to the parallelism in training ML algorithms, while maintaining the same deterministic output results. The execution time of the experiments was improved by a speedup of up to 2.2 when running on an 8 core CPU.

Keywords: Distributed Computing · Machine Learning · Intrusion Detection Systems

1 Introduction

Internet of Everything (IoE) is now seen as a young term that is not widely known yet and can be described as the next stage of the Internet of Things (IoT) or a superset of IoT, which is a machine-to-machine phenomenon. It connects people to people, machine-to-machine and people-to-machine systems [8].

IoE ecosystems although bringing a lot of benefits for society it also present ongoing cybersecurity challenges [16] that must be addressed to maintain the CIA triad - Confidentiality, Integrity, and Availability [11]. People are used to the internet and it must be as easy to use as possible but with the evolution

© ICST Institute for Computer Sciences, Social Informatics and Telecommunications Engineering 2024
Published by Springer Nature Switzerland AG 2024. All Rights Reserved
T. Pereira et al. (Eds.): IOECON 2023, LNICST 551, pp. 66–75, 2024.
https://doi.org/10.1007/978-3-031-51572-9_6

of IoT and IoE, the concerns are bigger. The impact of data loss or any other intervention can be crucial for critical systems such as Medical systems where the data must be protected and accessed for only those who are authorized, uneditable, and available anytime to be used [11].

A solution in a variety set of techniques of cybersecurity is the use of Intrusion Detection Systems (IDS) or Intrusion Prevention Systems (IPS) that use Artificial Intelligence to find attacks from unauthorized third parties [3]. IDS have an important role in the network infrastructure because they represent a layer of security that is able to detect a potential attack going on through the analysis of passing network traffic, in real-time, and to raise a warning about a specific threat.

Jamalipour and Mourali divide IDS into three categories: IDS based on Intrusion Data Sources, IDS based on Detection Techniques, and IDS based on Placement Strategies [5]. IDS Based on Intrusion Data Sources can be divided into Host-based IDSs (HIDS) and Network-based IDSs (NIDS). The HIDS are useful to detect attacks that do not contain network traffic such as databases, operating systems, or software logs. The NIDS are used in the network environment in order to analyse the network traffic and detect attacks.

IDS Based on Detection Techniques can be divided into four categories that make use of four different techniques. They can be Signature-Based IDS that consists in comparing the network traffic with a pre-defined signature or pattern. Another technique is Anomaly-Based IDS which consists of pre-defined standards of what is benign or malign based on network protocols and it is very efficient in the detection of malign but it can't detect what type of attack is. Specification-Based IDS are based on rules and thresholds set by experts which is similar to anomaly-based but the, in this case, the rules are applied based on someone's expertise. Finally, Hybrid-Based IDS combines both the signature-based and the anomaly-based, that is, the trade-off between the storage cost of the signature-based technique and the computing cost of the anomaly-based technique which is the best of "two worlds".

IDS Based on Placement Strategies can be divided into centralized IDS, distributed IDS, and hybrid IDS. Centralized IDS is placed either at the root node or a strategic node and analyzes the data traffic that is passing through to detect attacks. Distributed IDS Placement is a system of IDS where every node in the network will be configured with a full IDS taking advantage of a full analysis in each node preventing not only attacks from outside of the network and also inside the network. Hybrid IDS Placement combines both where there is a central IDS which is more capable of analyzing large amounts of data and a variety of lightweight nodes scattered in the network with less detection ratio but enough for the task needed.

When designing a Network Intrusion Detection System (NIDS) based on Machine Learning algorithms, the existence of previous data on attack types and their characteristics is of major importance to the success in the classification of the results, i.e., the capacity to distinguish between benign from malign (attack) packets. There are already some well-known datasets for NIDS, that cover a large variety of attack types, such as CICIDS-2017 [14], KDD [6], NSL-KDD [17] and UNSW-NB15 [13] and the most recent, HIKARI-2021 [4]. The NIDS's datasets that focus on network traffic have a large number of entries and features. The metadata from a simple packet crossing the network can be considerable in size and most of the mentioned datasets start with 50 or more features and some of the datasets have more than 500 000 entries.

Besides the importance of having a good amount of data to train an accurate NIDS, it is also important to choose the best model. There are several previous studies using traditional Machine Learning [2,3] and also Deep Learning [7,10] algorithms that address these problems. Nevertheless, it is always a question of balance between computation power and time to get the best model possible. Given enough resources, a developer would like to train each ML or DL model on each dataset, multiple times (to make sure the model is reliable), and adapt the hyper-parameters to make the final model more accurate. This work presents a simple approach to improve the existing computing capability when training different classification models with large datasets, in the context of cybersecurity, through the use of a distributed computing framework, Ray [12].

Ray is a distributed framework based on the Actor-model, where actors (entities with behavior) are capable of communicating with one another by sending and receiving messages in a shared-nothing distributed environment. This design facilitates the deployment of actors either at a single host, possibly where each actor is mapped to a CPU core, or across multiple hosts, where each actor is placed at a different host. Since actors can only communicate through message exchange, either by sending or receiving messages, in a shared-nothing distributed setup, this design permits the flexible deployment of a solution that can be adapted to a single host multi-core deployment, or into a multiple host possible multi-core deployment.

The use of this distributed platform maintains the previous objective of selecting the best possible model from a large number of experiments. Considering the design flexibility of adapting the solution into a concurrent setup, either through multiple cores on a single host, or by running multiple hosts, one expects the total execution time of multiple experiments to decrease by taking advantage of the multi-core and possibly multiple host resources that are already available but may not be efficiently used. This framework is a clean and simple approach to parallel the execution of computing tasks with minimal source code change, using the Python programming language and its multiple ML libraries like SciKit.

The paper is organised as follows: the next section presents the Related Work, the Machine Learning Models section presents the classification algorithms and the architecture for the distributed framework, the Results and Discussion section shows the results obtained with the experiments and the last section concludes our work.

2   Related Work

With the advent of Big Data, distributed computing frameworks were developed for executing code in a distributed setting. Apache Spark [15] was one of the first frameworks, based in the Java programming language, that could distribute code across multiple hosts, so that datasets with a size larger than the capacity of a single machine could be stored on a cluster of machines, and its parts processed concurrently at each host simultaneously. Spark offers a library of ML algorithms, designed specifically for the platform.

Another framework based in the Python programming language is Dask [1], which like Spark, is dataset oriented, i.e., the data from the dataset is partitioned and distributed across multiple hosts, and code is run at each partition concurrently to obtain computation results. The development of this framework was specifically suited for ML libraries like SciKit and other numerical libraries like NumPy.

Ray [12], in turn, is a Python framework based on the actor-model which consists on a set of actors (entities with generic computing capabilities) that can process any type of data locally, and communicate exclusively through messages. Although an actor-model generic framework is not designed to run machine learning algorithms efficiently, its generic design and flexibility enables it to be adapted to any computing requirement. In the case of this work, the execution of some ML algorithms using (single host) Python based ML libraries.

The use of a distributed platform to improve ML or DL algorithms has been used previously by other authors. Zhu et al. [19] describe an approach of efficient training of deep forests, a Deep Learning algorithm, on distributed task-parallel platforms where they compared Tensorflow and Ray, and by choosing Ray as the best platform to use, they were able to outperform another algorithm described in the paper with 7x to 20.9x speedup using a cluster of 16 nodes running in the Ray architecture.

Teixeira et al. [18] propose a new architecture of a hybrid IDS consisting in a central IDS where multiple algorithms are trained with multiple datasets and a IDS per company which is a result of the best model trained by the central IDS. The edge node IDS receives updates to the model itself and returns logs of classified traffic back to the central node/IDS. Ray was used to distribute tasks by the available resources.

3   Machine Learning Models

The use of a Machine Learning model to support the IDS classification problem requires the selection of one of multiple classification algorithms that were previously proposed in the literature [2]. Additionally, datasets must be considered for the training of the model. Finally, the configuration used to distribute the computing of the training phase of the classification algorithms is presented.

3.1 Classification Algorithms

There are multiple classification algorithms available from popular ML libraries: the K-Nearest-Neighbors (KNN), the Multi-Layer Perception (MLP), the Support Vector Machine (SVM classifier), the Random Forest (RF), the Decision Tree, the Gaussian, and the Logistic Regression. The library used to train these models was the scikit-learn using default parameters. The choosing of the most suitable algorithm is made by experimenting the multiple possibilities and to compare the results.

These classification algorithms will be evaluated with the following metrics: Accuracy and Precision. Accuracy is calculated by dividing the number of correctly identified predictions, true positives and true negatives, by the total number of predictions which means that by having a high accuracy the algorithm can be more trusted to classify the traffic. Precision is calculated by dividing the number of correctly identified malicious predictions, true positives, by the total number of predictions that the algorithm classified as malicious, true positives + false positive, which means that high precision is valuable to say that we can correctly identify the different type of malicious traffic.

3.2 Dataset

The dataset chosen for this experiment was the CICIDS-2017 [14]. It was already widely studied showing that it can be used as a dataset of reference in IDS problems. It contains both benign and malign traffic which resembles true real-world data (PCAPs). The dataset already contains some analysis provided by a network analyzer, CICFlowMeter, and it was saved as a CSV file publicly accessed.

The dataset has a total of 80 features, both numerical and categorical, and more than 2 million entries and it is classified as benign or malign (Brute Force FTP, Brute Force SSH, DoS, Heartbleed, Web Attack, Infiltration, Botnet, and DDoS).

Several researchers have studied this dataset, Kurniabudi et al. affirm that the number of features used from the dataset affects the execution time [9].

In this case, we decided to use only 20% of the dataset, choosing 20% of each label so that we can use a balanced dataset, and using all the features so we can see the worst scenario in training time.

3.3 Distributed Training

The experiments necessary to perform this study consist in a number of classification algorithms applied to IDS specific datasets. Thorough studies make use of several algorithms with several datasets. For this demonstration, seven algorithms will be applied to one dataset. This setting, although small, is sufficient to make the proof of concept and demonstrate how a distributed framework using the actor-model can be applied to parallelise ML algorithms.

————————————— Sequential ——————————————   ————————————— Parallel (Ray) —————————————

```
def runRF():                                            @ray.remote
    model = RandomForestClassifier(random_state=1)      def runRF(num_CPU=1):
    model.fit( CDS.X_train, CDS.Y_train)                    model = RandomForestClassifier(random_state = 1)
    Y_predict = model.predict(CDS.X_test)                   model.fit( CDS.X_train, CDS.Y_train)
    accuracy = accuracy_score(CDS.Y_test, Y_predict)        Y_predict = model.predict(CDS.X_test)
                                                            accuracy = accuracy_score(CDS.Y_test, Y_predict)
```

Fig. 1. Code snippets for the Sequential and Parallel (Ray) versions

The usual classification pipeline starts with the training of the model with the dataset, which is a costly operation, and then testing to assess performance indicators. Our purpose is to speed up the training phase of each model. Two approaches are available to parallelise the training phase. We can approach the parallelisation of each algorithm internal execution (low-level approach), or we can parallelise the algorithm as an independent task regarding the others (high-level approach). We opted to follow the later design due to its simplicity and for not requiring knowledge on specific implementation details of the inner workings of each algorithm.

Each pair algorithm-dataset will form a task (following Ray terminology), which represents an actor. The distributed system will be made of multiple tasks, each one running on an available processor. Since each algorithm shares nothing with the other algorithms, the mapping between the algorithms and the tasks (actors) on the platform is perfect. Each task may then run at its own pace. The experiments are concluded when all tasks have finished their execution and all performance indicators can be gathered from all algorithms, so that a decision can be made regarding the best ML model.

Ray, following the actor-model, makes it very easy to adapt traditional sequential Python code for a parallel distributed environment. The Fig. 1 shows two code snippets, the first represents a typical sequential design, and the second presents the parallel enabled version. As it can be observed, the code changes are minimal: an annotation indicating the function will be deployed as a Ray task, and the launch of the Ray platform through a main call to ray.init(). The deployment of this code is automatically handled by the Ray platform, i.e., launching instances for each available processor at each host in the Ray cluster, and executing each task remotely.

4   Results and Discussion

Considering as the starting point the execution of seven classification algorithms with the CICIDS dataset, our objective is to compare the impact of multiple processors when running a set of experiments. In order to do so, the Ray framework will be used, and have each algorithm to be run as an (independent) task.

Our study will look at the impact of having multiple processors, starting with the single processor case (1P - 1 CPU), and increasing the number of processors (2P, 4P, 8P - 2,4,8 CPU), on performance indicators, namely the global execution time. All experiments were run on a single machine with an Intel(R) Core(TM) i5-12400F CPU with 6 threads, 12 logical processors, with 16 Gb of RAM. The code was executed in Python 3.10, scikit-learn 1.2.2, and ray 2.3.1. Although just one host was used in this experiments, the design of the actor-model enables this same setup to be scaled into a cluster of hosts without any modification in the source code. The difference would be to setup a Ray cluster with all the member hosts.

In order to prove that the distributed experiments work well in multiple execution runs we designed the application to load the dataset and partition it using the same deterministic approach, so that executions are reproducible. By applying this setting we can run the same algorithm twice or more and get always the same metrics of evaluation.

Table 1. Results of the Distributed ML experience

Algorithm	Accuracy	Precision	Time (1P)	Time (2P)	Time (4P)	Time (8P)
KNN	0.990	0.990	254.045	270.987	306.704	311.024
Decision Tree	0.998	0.998	16.782	17.190	20.116	33.768
MLP	0.984	0.984	322.267	323.247	356.048	363.865
SVC	0.955	0.955	106.347	103.193	146.305	146.327
Random Forest	0.998	0.998	85.685	87.451	118.002	133.030
Linear Regression	0.948	0.944	23.561	25.004	30.781	35.644
Gaussian	0.712	0.971	3.176	3.277	3.987	4.375

Sum of the individual time	557.819	559.362	675.237	717.010
Total execution time	817.857	565.374	381.960	370.588
Speedup	1	1.447	2.141	2.207

Table 1 shows the results of the experiments described before. In these results, we can compare the algorithms with the accuracy, precision, and execution time needed to train (in seconds). The labels 1P, 2P, 4P and 8P refer to the number of CPU used.

By comparing the accuracy and precision in each execution run we can verify that the results are always the same for each algorithm which means that our implementation is deterministic. These results are not shown but were validated.

Although deterministic on the accuracy and precision metrics, the execution time of each run changes slightly for the different CPU settings. The code executed was always the same, and this fluctuation on the execution time can be attributed to Ray's internal management of tasks. The total sum of each individual experiment was slightly different from the others, and includes this internal Ray management.

We can see that if we run the entire experiment in sequence (1P experiment) the time needed to train all the algorithms is 817 s. By comparing the four values of the total execution time needed to train in each experiment we can see that

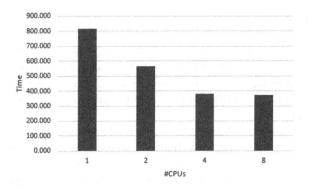

Fig. 2. Execution time vs Number of CPU)

there is a correlation between the number of CPU and the time needed. By increasing the number of CPU we reduce the time needed to train.

This result is expected since tasks are parallelised, when adding one more CPU, we add the simultaneous execution of one more actor. Although the sum of all individual times does not reduce, since the calculations are the same, the final execution time reduces, because we increased parallelism.

On the other side, we can notice a reduction of time between 2P and 4P which is 183.414 s, and between 4P and 8P which is 11.372 s. The difference between the 4P and 8P cases is smaller than the one obtained between the 2P and the 4P cases. This is due to the fact that we have only 7 tasks, but have available 8 processors. When the level of parallelism reaches the number of actors, the execution time converges to the highest individual task execution time, i.e., all tasks finish before the longest lasting but the application only finishes when all tasks are over.

In this experiment, the individual execution times differ significantly between one another. The fastest task takes 3 s (for the P1 case) and the longest task takes 322 s (for the P1 case). This high variation becomes noticeable when the number of processors increases up to the number of tasks, making the total execution time equals the time of the longest execution individual task.

The metrics of comparison of those experiments was speedup. Speedup is determined by dividing the sequential time of execution by the parallel time of execution for each experiment. We can confirm that distributed computing works well in this case because we see an increase in speedup when increasing the number of CPU. The best result occurs when using 8 CPU (8P), achieving a speedup of 2,2.

The impact of the number of CPU on the reduction of time can be seen in Fig. 2. It shows a descent tendency on the global execution time as the number of processors grow, more accentuated in the first experiments and less in the last, as explained before.

5   Conclusion

Overall this work represents an approach to distributed computing, using Ray, for running ML algorithms in IDS problems. With this approach, we were able to train seven different algorithms concurrently and by comparing the experiments with different numbers of CPU we were able to say that by using 8 CPU we can achieve a speedup of 2.2.

Our results show that it is indeed very simple and straightforward to adapt sequential Python code to run in a distributed setup. Secondly, the performance results show that even a single desktop machine with multi-core processor can speedup the execution of multiple simulations. Finally, this approach reveals itself adequate to scale a high number of experiments into a cluster of hosts with relative simplicity.

The findings of this research allow researchers to improve the process of training ML algorithms with a high number of experiments to be made, where time is crucial to make decisions.

As future work we plan to introduce more datasets and more algorithms, increasing the number of tasks to parallelise, and to quantify the effective speedup at a large scale cluster.

Acknowledgments. This work was funded by the project "Cybers SeC IP" (NORTE-01-0145-FEDER-000044), supported by Northern Portugal Regional Operational Programme (Norte2020), under the Portugal 2020 Partnership Agreement, through the European Regional Development Fund (ERDF).

References

1. Dask. https://www.dask.org/
2. Fernandes, R., Lopes, N.: Network intrusion detection packet classification with the hikari-2021 dataset: a study on ml algorithms. In: 2022 10th International Symposium on Digital Forensics and Security (ISDFS), pp. 1–5 (2022). https://doi.org/10.1109/ISDFS55398.2022.9800807
3. Fernandes, R., Silva, J., Ribeiro, O., Portela, I., Lopes, N.: The impact of identifiable features in ML classification algorithms with the HIKARI-2021 dataset. In: 2023 11th International Symposium on Digital Forensics and Security (ISDFS), pp. 1–5 (2023). https://doi.org/10.1109/ISDFS58141.2023.10131864
4. Ferriyan, A., Thamrin, A.H., Takeda, K., Murai, J.: Generating network intrusion detection dataset based on real and encrypted synthetic attack traffic. Appl. Sci. **11**(17), 7868 (2021). https://doi.org/10.3390/app11177868
5. Jamalipour, A., Murali, S.: A taxonomy of machine-learning-based intrusion detection systems for the internet of things: a survey. IEEE Internet Things J. **9**(12), 9444–9466 (2022). https://doi.org/10.1109/JIOT.2021.3126811
6. KDD Cup 1999 Data. http://kdd.ics.uci.edu/databases/kddcup99/kddcup99.html
7. Khan, R.U., Zhang, X., Alazab, M., Kumar, R.: An improved convolutional neural network model for intrusion detection in networks. In: 2019 Cybersecurity and Cyberforensics Conference (CCC), pp. 74–77 (2019). https://doi.org/10.1109/CCC.2019.000-6

8. Kiesler, N., Impagliazzo, J.: Perspectives on the internet of everything. In: Pereira, T., Impagliazzo, J., Santos, H. (eds.) Internet of Everything, pp. 3–17. Springer Nature Switzerland, Cham (2023). https://doi.org/10.1007/978-3-031-25222-8_1

9. Stiawan, D., Idris, M.Y.B., Bamhdi, A.M., Budiarto, R.: CICIDS-2017 dataset feature analysis with information gain for anomaly detection. IEEE Access **8**, 132911–132921 (2020). https://doi.org/10.1109/ACCESS.2020.3009843

10. Latif, S., Zou, Z., Idrees, Z., Ahmad, J.: A novel attack detection scheme for the industrial internet of things using a lightweight random neural network. IEEE Access **8**, 89337–89350 (2020). https://doi.org/10.1109/ACCESS.2020.2994079

11. Longras, A., Pereira, T., Amaral, A.: Cybersecurity challenges in healthcare medical devices. In: Pereira, T., Impagliazzo, J., Santos, H. (eds.) Internet of Everything, pp. 66–75. Springer Nature Switzerland, Cham (2023). https://doi.org/10.1007/978-3-031-25222-8_6

12. Moritz, P., et al.: Ray: a distributed framework for emerging AI applications (2018)

13. Moustafa, N., Slay, J.: UNSW-NB15: a comprehensive data set for network intrusion detection systems (UNSW-NB15 network data set). In: 2015 Military Communications and Information Systems Conference (MilCIS), pp. 1–6 (2015). https://doi.org/10.1109/MilCIS.2015.7348942

14. Sharafaldin, I., Lashkari, A.H., Ghorbani, A.A.: Toward generating a new intrusion detection dataset and intrusion traffic characterization. In: International Conference on Information Systems Security and Privacy (2018)

15. Apache spark. https://spark.apache.org/

16. Stavrou, E.: Guidelines to develop consumers cyber resilience capabilities in the ioe ecosystem. In: Pereira, T., Impagliazzo, J., Santos, H. (eds.) Internet of Everything, pp. 18–28. Springer Nature Switzerland, Cham (2023). https://doi.org/10.1007/978-3-031-25222-8_2

17. Tavallaee, M., Bagheri, E., Lu, W., Ghorbani, A.A.: A detailed analysis of the KDD CUP 99 data set. In: 2009 IEEE Symposium on Computational Intelligence for Security and Defense Applications, pp. 1–6 (2009). https://doi.org/10.1109/CISDA.2009.5356528

18. Teixeira, D., Malta, S., Pinto, P.: A vote-based architecture to generate classified datasets and improve performance of intrusion detection systems based on supervised learning. Future Internet **14**(3), 72 (2022). https://doi.org/10.3390/fi14030072

19. Zhu, G., Hu, Q., Gu, R., Yuan, C., Huang, Y.: ForestLayer: efficient training of deep forests on distributed task-parallel platforms. J. Parallel Distrib. Comput. **132**, 113–126 (2019). https://doi.org/10.1016/j.jpdc.2019.05.001

Exploring Risk Analysis Methods in IoE Projects: A Smart Campus Use Case

Henrique Santos[(✉)] and Tiago Pereira

Universidade do Minho, Centro Algoritmi, Guimarães, Portugal
{hsantos,tcpereira}@dsi.uminho.pt

Abstract. The IoT is an ICT development paradigm based on technological evolution. The underlying vision is an increasingly sensorized world, where all phenomena can be virtually digitised and processed by machines, interacting to improve humanity's quality of life. This transformation has taken place at breakneck speed. In a few years, the Internet began to be mainly used by machines, whose number and variety have increased exponentially, in symbiosis with humans, giving rise to the Internet of Everything (IoE) concept. Among the challenges in pursuing this primary objective, information security is one of the most relevant. Security flaws imply a loss of trust, compromising the acceptance and use of the entire system. Analysing risks and anticipating problems is imperative for any project in this field. However, the traditional risk analysis (RA) methods aiming at isolated Information Systems must be revised, given the complexity and dependence between systems in the IoE. Furthermore, traditional RA is performed periodically, usually annually, while the threat landscape linked to IoE changes more rapidly, demanding new approaches. This paper presents a survey of RA methods that have been applied in this context, justifying and demonstrating their adjustments to a particular case of a Smart Campus project. The results demonstrate the method's usefulness for planning adequate techniques to achieve the security-by-design and by-default principle.

Keywords: IoT · IoE · Risk Analysis · Risk Assessment · Smart Campus · Cybersecurity

1 Introduction

With the accelerated evolution of ICT in the last decade, we have witnessed many notable evolution. Computer networks, computing systems and intelligent software platforms have generated an ecosystem that today creates the illusion that we have the best and most accurate information available, anywhere and whenever we need it. The Internet of Things (IoT) was a term coined in first place

Supported by Lab4U&Spaces – Living Lab of Interactive Urban Space Solution, Ref. NORTE-01-0145-FEDER-000072, financed by community funds (FEDER), through Norte 2020.

T. Pereira et al. (Eds.): IOECON 2023, LNICST 551, pp. 76–91, 2024.
https://doi.org/10.1007/978-3-031-51572-9_7

to describe a view of this evolution, emphasising that the Internet space, until then focused on use by humans, was beginning to be exposed to use by machines, thanks to a set of emerging specific protocols, called machine-to-machine (M2M) [2,5,8,15]. In fact, according to well-known surveys, sometime in mid-2018, the number of 'things' using the Internet surpassed the number of human beings, and since then, it has grown in a sustained way without indications of slowing down [42]. One of the key transformations in this process was the adoption of the IPv6 protocol, which makes it possible to extend the Internet to millions of devices per square centimetre of the Earth's surface [39].

A natural next step was to merge both worlds, taking advantage of AI techniques and a massive amount of information, as well as processing and storage power, opening doors to adopting the term Internet of Everything (IoE). The vision is to have machines and humans cooperating to improve the quality of life on the planet. Some other terms emerged, such as the Internet of Nano Things (IoNT), to highlight the possibility of integrating sub micron-scale devices, which IPv6 allows and promotes [35]. One of the most prominent applications is in the health area, with the so-called Body Area Networks (BAN) [16].

Among the vast range of applications, the smart spaces has deserved much attention. The tendency to increase the concentration of people in urban spaces and the need to guarantee high quality of life standards pose serious challenges, mainly at the policy and government levels. Additionally, the need to better manage spaces has been markedly evidenced by the most recent COVID-19 pandemic crises and extreme weather events [25]. In the space of supporting solutions ICT and AI play a crucial role. The increase in research works and projects in Smart Cities, Smart Agriculture, and Smart Industries, among many other smart-like applications, is a clear sign of this [19,21,31]. Academic campuses are no exception. Following the generalised trend, some research works have been addressing the issues of this specific type of space, referred to as Smart Campus (SCampus). Concerning technological infrastructure shares identical solutions type with, for instance, Smart Cities. The main differences are in the focus and specific functions implemented. Most proposed models define six development dimensions: environment, energy, management, social, educational services, and utilities. Applications in each domain handle data from myriad linked sensors and sources, perform some intelligent analysis, and output results to proper operators' dashboards to better support decision-making [14,34].

SCampus involves innovative technology and people (students, staff, and general public), which are crucial for its main operation and (in)success. In most studies related to smart space challenges, security and privacy emerge as fundamental properties demanding proper management [11,17]. In addition to the different, complex and new technology stacks that support IoE and SCampus, we have a vast universe of very heterogeneous users regarding ICT awareness and expertise in its use. Even with the best security and privacy controls in place, uncertainty and mistrust can compromise the functional goals of any SCampus project. Thus, risk and trust assume a particularly relevant role and must be adequately addressed, on an ongoing basis, throughout the project's entire life cycle [13, 41].

Security and privacy impositions are non-functional requirements for projects. By definition, this type of requirement imposes restrictions on flexibility and general functional requirements, which are the base of the business model and, at large, of its success. So, in general, security and privacy may limit the exploitation of a product to the limit of making it unusable. Nevertheless, ignoring security and privacy issues can definitely damage the product's reputation, with the same final consequence. Finding the right balance is a challenging goal defined under a risk management process [39]. Each application domain and deployment restrictions imply different approaches concerning both technology and human resources. Furthermore, the risk perception of different communities makes it even harder to find some widely accepted security solutions. This is why the security area has been supported mainly by standards, sometimes focused on specific domains, trying to capitalise on the knowledge of experts to find a good solution. Smart Cities are no exception being possible to identify a framework of dedicated standards [32]. The number of security and privacy standards available is already significant, making it difficult to decide which ones to use [40]. Nevertheless, most standards and good practices guides defend an approach based on the Risk Management process. In this paper we will address the issues of trying to apply a Risk Analysis approach, and in particular Risk Assessment, to a project within the SCampus domain, named Lab4USpaces.

The paper is structured as follows: Sect. 2 present the fundamental concepts related to Information Security that are used along the paper, including the Risk Analysis model; Sect. 3 discuss the related work, emphasising the use of the ATT&CK matrix for threat modelling; Sect. 4 describes in detail each of the three steps of the proposed model (system description, threat modelling, and impact assessment), using as a case study a research project aiming at developing a Smart Campus – Lab4USpaces; finally, Sect. 5 draws some conclusions related to the applicability of the proposed model and refer the future work.

2   Fundamental Concepts

Before approaching the models and techniques already developed for risk management in the environment in question, it is convenient to define some fundamental concepts. We will use the ISO/IEC 27000 standard as a reference, although any text that addresses this topic presents similar definitions. The main concepts (in a simplified way) are [39]:

Information Security It is a process aiming to preserve a given set of properties or objectives relevant to information security; more specifically, it aims at the *"preservation of confidentiality, integrity and availability of information"* [27, pp. 6]:
  – **Integrity**, to ensure information **is not modified** or **created** in an undesirable way;

- **Confidentiality**, to ensure information **is available only** to legitimate subjects;
- **Availability**, to ensure information **is available** whenever we need it; and
- **Others**, which is a placeholder for properties deriving from the above three, whenever security objectives are more specific; this is particularly relevant with integrity and confidentiality since the concepts are too abstract (e.g., assuring ownership and authenticity is probably critical for healthcare information, and both are related to integrity).

Threat A **possible cause of damage** in one or more security properties. When analysing threats it is possible not be aware of their origin, or how an accident might occur. Threats are frequently linked to security properties. However, they can also arise from the perception of the existence of an Information System's weaknesses, or even dangerous situations from the environment.

Attack Any malicious action or group of actions, intentional or not, that will **offend one or more security properties**, causing some harm to the Information System. Attacks may be executed by external or internal agents. When analysing possible attacks, we usually start with a relevant threat and in all possible ways it can be came into effect.

Vulnerability Any **flaw** or **weakness** existing in the Information System, which can be explored by a possible attack.

Resource Any asset that has **value** to the organisation. Knowing that value is crucial to define the impact of a total or partial loss. With intangible resources it is a considerable challenge to define it.

Risk Result of **uncertainty on security objectives**, when the Information System faces deviations from the correct behaviour. Uncertainty is related to a deficit of knowledge about events, their consequences or likelihood. Given the nature and variety of the events, that deficit may be impossible to overcome.

Security Controls All the measures we can take to **manage the risk**. It includes **policies, guidelines, procedures, and practices**. Their nature can be **administrative, technical, management, or legal**. Frequently, they are also referenced by safeguards or countermeasures. The ISO/IEC Standard 27001 [26] defines 14 security controls' classes, linked to 34 security objectives and a total of 124 specific controls. About half of those controls address technical issues, while the other group address organisational issues. Despite the relevance of this standard, there is no general consensus about its benefits. Frameworks like the SP 800-53 [36], or the CIS Critical Security Controls (CIS Controls) [1], among a few others usually promoted by specific companies selling security related services, are frequently considered useful alternatives.

2.1 Risk Analysis Model

The relationships between those concepts are highlighted in Fig. 1a, and establish a simple Risk Analysis model [39]. While the detailed analysis of this model is out of scope, it is important to highlight some aspects. The three elements related to hazards (threats, attacks, and vulnerabilities) should allow us to derive the likelihood of any malicious action. Combining it with the resources' impact value, allows us to assess the risk, which must be the basis to choose the proper security controls. While impact value is intrinsic to each organisation and must be agreed upon within it, the threat landscape, particularly the attack techniques diversity, presents a primary challenge to recognise the second risk component. Attack modelling has been the target of several studies and solutions, but even so, it is still missing a practical approach limiting applicability in real world [10].

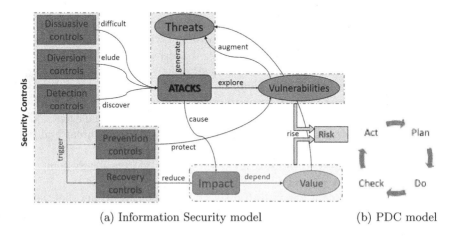

(a) Information Security model   (b) PDC model

Fig. 1. Basic models for Information Security

Despite the simplicity of the above model, the lack of systematised knowledge regarding security and privacy threats and objectives, or even about security controls' efficiency, raises many uncertainties ameliorated only by the adoption of a continuous cycle model aiming to improve the security function over time – usually referred as the PDC (Plan, Do Check, and Act) model shown in Fig. 1b. This model characterises the Information Security function as a **management process**, referred by ISMS (Information Security Management System) [27]. Behind this simple formulation lies a considerable difficulty in finding the appropriate metrics to assess security (phase Check) with a view of its management. Finally, and still looking at Fig. 1a, the classification adopted for the security controls only partially aligns with the abovementioned standards. It focuses on the purpose towards threats from five alternative perspectives: deterrence, illusion, detection, prevention and recovery [39]. Each class exhibits a particular level of implementation cost and efficacy expectation, impacting the required monitoring level and the linked metrics.

Although it may currently be considered unthinkable not to implement an ISMS in any organisation that depends minimally on its IS, several factors condition its implementation. In [22], the authors suggest that limited resources and the need for alignment with business goals can make it challenging to establish and operate all involved processes at the same level of maturity. In [45], the authors refer to top management support, resource planning, competency development, and awareness as critical points. The main difficulties can be attributed to the need for more preparation and awareness or less commitment from the people involved. Nevertheless, the increasing complexity of IT systems makes it also challenging for security practitioners to filter out the noise and focus on the essential threats, impacting their apparent competency [18] – in this last work, the authors also suggests that a systematic approach to identifying and documenting security threats is necessary.

3   Related Work

Risk Analysis, particularly Risk Assessment, is always hard to perform in any environment. In some cases, it is imperative to do so (e.g., critical systems or health systems); in others, there may even be regulatory or legal impositions (e.g., financial sector, in the USA), but in the vast majority of applications, it ends up being the market and users that may demand more or less in terms of security and privacy. A SCampus fits this last perspective. Some standards can be followed, but there are no mandatory rules or system certifications [3]. There are some system design recommendations, but typically they are not intended to be used by such heterogeneous communities, where some individuals are aware of the hazards and others are not. Even so, some interesting works focus on Risk Analysis in that environment type.

Towards an effective Risk Analysis process, the first step consists of identifying and characterising the threat landscape (if we cannot identify what can damage our IS, we cannot defend it), the main assets, and deriving a risk value (Risk Assessment). In [29], the authors discuss several types of attacks that can threaten a Smart Environment based on IoT. However, there are no clear security objectives or indicators allowing detection and effect measuring, limiting the practicability of the approach. Exploring different approaches, [44] proposes using the EBIOS methodology to identify weaknesses and vulnerabilities in IoT architectures, while [43] presents a survey and proposes a taxonomy of security Risk Assessment methodologies. In [30], the authors propose a multi-dimensional security Risk Assessment model based on three elements: assets, threats, and vulnerabilities. In a bottom-up approach, [33] conducts a systematic literature review to analyse the security of IoT devices and proposes using mobile computing to address security challenges and provide potential solutions. Overall, all these works suggest that traditional security Risk Assessment methodologies may not be effective in the IoT and SCampus context, and that new approaches are needed to address the unique challenges.

More specifically oriented to SCampus (or Smart Cities), but clearly still in a generalist approach, [9] propose some Risk Assessment techniques, including risk prediction and evaluation based on ISO27001 standards. It also suggests using data mining to identify information security threats in campus networks, such as database-related attacks. In [7], the authors focus on surveillance systems in IoT-enabled Smart Campuses, proposing a taxonomy and weighted scoring model to assess the state-of-the-art systems. Meanwhile, in [24], the authors propose an information security Risk Assessment model, which includes 20 risk factors from five domains: infrastructure, data service, information content, information management, and public literacy. The model uses the decision tree algorithm to assess information security risks. Additionally, [28] proposes a comprehensive method for automatic security management of smart infrastructures using attack graphs and risk analysis. In synthesis, most of the above works assume that security objectives and threats are well-known or easy to identify, which is a fallacy as this knowledge can rarely be consolidated in the community of all stakeholders (including users).

There are already well-known models for studying attacks. However, these models are very focused on the study of attacks rather than their role in Risk Analysis, where the concern is not how the attack is executed but more on the effects and exploitation opportunities that can impact the system. A possible approach to address this gap is to use the MITRE ATT&CK matrix (Adversarial Tactics, Techniques, and Common Knowledge). In simple terms, it is a database with strategies (attacker goals), techniques and effects of cyberattacks, to which is added information on how to detect, mitigate, and even some examples of its use and groups of hackers that use or have used it. The matrix has been built by an open community, and has become a useful conceptual tool across many cybersecurity disciplines to convey threat intelligence, perform testing through red teaming or adversary emulation, and improve network and system defenses against intrusions [12].

Concerning specifically Risk Assessment, the ATT&CK matrix has already shown some virtues. In [20], the authors present research results on associating a comprehensive set of organisational and individual culture factors with security vulnerabilities mapped to specific adversary behaviour and patterns. Other relevant results are reported in [6] that proposes a new risk assessment approach based on a Failure Modes Effects and Criticality Analysis (FMECA) that is enriched with selected semantics and components of the MITRE ATT&ACK framework; [37] applies the framework to assess security risks of an integrated navigation system (INS) on a vessel; and [23] proposes an IS risk assessment method based on the ATT&CK model, which can calculate the risk value of security threats caused by various attack tactics and techniques, to effectively determine the risk indicator that should be paid attention to when the information system is under security threat.

The works mentioned above demonstrate the usefulness of the ATT&CK matrix and several ways it can be used for Risk Assessment. Nevertheless, there are some works whose results influence more directly the work described in this paper. In [38], the authors provide an extensive systematic review and a taxonomy of the applications and research on ATT&CK. Concerning Risk Assessment – one of the approached use cases – it identifies some works where the authors complement other frameworks (e.g., ISO/IEC 27005, NIST SP800-30) with ATT&CK to enrich the risk perception and impact effectively. Notwithstanding, it also highlights the need for more research on the practical implementation and evaluation of ATT&CK. A relevant example of the complimentary between Risk Analysis frameworks and the ATT&CK matrix is given in [4]. The authors begin by identifying implementation models defined by the reference frameworks and then explore the semantic richness of the ATT&CK matrix to conduct the risk assessment. Among the implementation models, the Asset/Impact-centric approach assumes particular relevance here. It is used when adversaries, vulnerabilities and group threats are challenging to recognise or when assets are considered more critical. As will be seen, this is the most appropriate framework for the Lab4USpaces project.

4   Proposed Solution

This section describes the work carried out to perform a Risk Analysis process on the Smart Campus research project called Lab4U&Spaces[1]. The project's primary goal is to explore innovative technologies to increase the university campus's quality of life. We decided to follow a similar method to the one adopted by [4], but without a deeper attack analysis since we envisage a limited exposition and a low level of interest for sophisticated attackers, being enough a qualitative estimation for risks. The focus is on understanding the threats and impacts, not on the attack variants and their mitigation. The Risk Analysis framework used is described in Sect. 2.1, complemented with the MITRE ATT&CK to deduce the qualitative risk level, as described next.

4.1   Step 1: System Description

The general system architecture proposed for the Lab4USpaces platform is organised in four layers, as usually adopted for this type of system. Figure 2 shows a high-level version of the architecture, highlighting the role of the four layers and the main components of each, with enough detail to understand their function, the relevant assets, and the subjects involved. When describing a system this way, we may expect to identify the main threats and probability of success to emerge, even if that is not the primary objective.

The physical layer encompasses several sensors and actuators, which generally interact with the environment. Here we can categorise the device types:

- Resource-limited devices, whose function cannot be modified on the fly; reprogramming demands special equipment or physical access, meaning there is no way of accessing them remotely. They are connected to the upper layer by wireless networks, and to preserve battery life, usually, they do not perform complex authentication and ciphering operations. The main threats are usually related to rogue devices and the openness of wireless networks. In the case of actuators controlling critical operations, or sensors capturing critical information, such as private data (e.g., health data), those threats can raise higher risks. Otherwise, risk should be low.

---

[1] https://transparencia.gov.pt/pt/fundos-europeus/beneficiarios-projetos/projeto/
NORTE-01-0145-FEDER-000072.

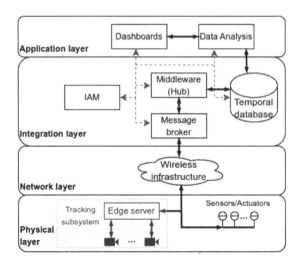

Fig. 2. Lab4USpaces platform general architecture

- Resource-limited programmable devices, whose function can be modified on the fly; this is a variant of the above, using powerful micro-controllers (e.g., ESP-32) that can be programmed remotely, through wireless, being exposed to malware; since they do not have an Operating System their functional capacity is limited, but so it is the support for any anti-malware or high sophisticated defence mechanism. Concerning security risks, the rationale above also applies, adding the exposition to remote tempering and abuse, with impact both at the data and network levels.
- Fully-capable computerised devices, like smartphones or laptop computers, serving as sensors or actuators, usually through dedicated applications. These devices face all the usual cyberthreats, possibly even being infected and abused. In the case of mobile devices using cellular communication technology, there is an additional threat related to exploiting that second channel as a gateway for networks outside our architecture.
- Edge computers, working as a hub for a set of related low-level devices, providing data pre-processing operations and/or a network node switching function for optimisation reasons. These are full-capable computers with the usual cyberthreats worsened by the use of wireless networks. Another aggravating factor is the non-interactive way it is used, making it difficult to observe anomalous behaviours that could trigger an alarm.

The network layer encompasses all the wireless access points, besides the network switches, firewalls and Intrusion Detection Systems that filter the traffic towards the upper level. Assuming they are properly configured, the main threat at this level is the wireless network and all its inherent vulnerabilities.

The integration layer resides in a private network and encompasses four main blocks:

- a message broker to properly organise the communication with the different low-level device classes;
- a temporal database as the central data repository;
- a middleware platform (at the moment, we are using Home Assistant) to provide sensors and actuators integration, visualisation, and simple data analysis functions; and
- an identity and access control management software (IAM) to implement Access Control functions for all users and devices capable of using OpenID connect and OAuth2 protocols. At the moment, we are using Keycloak.

All these components are isolated from the Internet, and all accesses are controlled using the best well-known protocols. So, even if we can consider a minimum risk, this is where the most valuable data is stored. Privacy issues can also become critical, as well as insider threats, since administrators and system operators will have access to the core components.

The application layer includes all software dedicated to high-level data analysis and dashboards. This is the only level within the architecture accessible to external users. Eventual external attacks will try to explore the link entry points at this level. Besides the user authentication and authorisation provided by the IAM, all system request should be filtered by a proxy or similar device at the entrance of the integration layer (not shown in Fig. 2).

From the above description and considering the role of each component, it is possible to identify the main assets and their potential impact on security properties. Table 1 synthesises that information. The impact is measured in three levels since it seems unnecessary to distinguish further the assets with higher impact at this stage. However, these assumptions may be reviewed later if necessary. The 'Exposition' column highlights the medium by which the assets can be reached, being the primary source of attacks. As expected, the wireless networks represent the main source of threads in the Lab4USpaces project. Still, to undertake a more accurate Risk Assessment, the threats must be explored more deeply.

4.2   Step 2: Threat Modelling

Threat modelling is an activity aiming to understand threats better. Most proposed methods focus on discovering how the related attacks are deployed, the tools used, and the explored vulnerabilities. This information is essential for mitigation purposes. However, from the initial Risk Assessment point of view, the main question is: How likely will it affect our system?

The ATT&CK matrix (see also Sect. 3) is a database that aggregates information about **tactics** (goals), **techniques, procedure examples, software tools, threat groups and campaigns, mitigation actions**, and **detectors' data sources**. The MITRE organisation also provides a front-end tool named ATT&CK Navigator[2] to explore the matrix and all the correlations between the

---

[2] https://mitre-attack.github.io/attack-navigator/.

Table 1. Asset/Impact synthesis.

Asset	Exposition	Impact	Notes
Resource-limited devices	None	Low	Should not be used with critical data/processes
Small programmable devices	Wireless	**High**	Remote control and data injection
Computer-like nodes	Wireless and cellular com	**High**	Data injection
Edge nodes	Wireless	Medium	Sensor devices integration
Network nodes	Wireless	**High**	Network devices integration
Message Broker	Limited	Low	Data publish and subscribe
Temporal Database	None	**High**	Central repository for all data
Middleware platform	None	Low	Integration rules and data filtering
IAM	None	Low	Authentication and authorisation information
Web applications	Internet	**High**	APIs for web applications

different dimensions. The Navigator allows extraction of partial views, named layers, based on a subset of tactics or techniques and using one of three domains: Enterprise, ICS (Industrial Control Systems), and Mobile. The first includes all tactics and techniques, while the others include a subset matching the indicated contexts. For illustration, the following steps describe how we approached the matrix, starting with the broader domain and searching for the Risk Assessment related details for some of the assets enumerated in Table 1:

1. In the architectural study, the wireless medium appears linked to the resources with the most significant impact. Using 'Wireless' as the search term, only three related techniques appear:
   - **Network Sniffing**, used for **Discovery** and **Credential Access** goals; reading the technique description and denoting a large number of Procedure Examples, it is evident that the medium and supporting protocols themselves are inherently vulnerable; we avoid credential abuse and data leakage by using cypher-based protocols; even so, the probability of a successful Network Sniffing attack is **very high**.
   - **Hardware Additions**, used for **Initial Access** goal; it consists of adding devices into the system or network; the Procedure Examples indicates just one case consisting of the addition of small computers, like Raspberry Pi, in a local network; looking into Fig. 2, especially at the physical layer and giving the sensors' diversity without the capacity to implement robust authentication mechanisms, the success of this attack is **very high**; at higher levels, the implementation of proper access control policies reduces the probability of successful attacks, but does not mitigate the threat.

- **Brute Force: Password Guessing**, used for (tactic or goal) Credential Access; the description and the high number of Procedure Examples reveal a severe challenge, mainly at the application layer, since at lower levels, most devices use tokens instead of passwords; as we will be using exposed protocols like SSH and HTTPS (despite being secure by robust ciphering techniques and a password policy) the success of these attacks are **high**.

2. The central repository also shows a high impact if it is possible to improperly take data (exfiltration) or to mess up data (manipulation).
   - Starting with **Exfiltration**, the ATT&CK includes a specific tactic for that goal, with nine techniques and some sub-techniques; one, in particular, is relevant in the context of the identified assets, **Exfiltration Over Web Service**, consisting of exploring eventual Web services' vulnerabilities; in this case, the Procedure Examples refer to existing cloud services, but giving the shared libraries, modules used, and server side languages when building Web services, most likely they will suffer from similar weaknesses, resulting in a **significant success probability** for this technique.

3. For the second data threat, searching the ATT&CK matrix for the term 'manipulation' within the description field returns 21 attack techniques; most of them are related to control operations, account abuse, or network and specific applications vulnerabilities, which do not fit the central repository case, but one technique stands out for the correspondence: **Data Manipulation: Stored Data Manipulation**; the corresponding tactic is **Impact**, denoting the destructive nature of the technique, but the limited Procedure Examples reveals its inherent limited efficacy; giving its potential impact, the probability of a successful attack is **very high**.

4.3   Step: 3: Impact Assessment

The final step consists on determining the risk value for each asset. The objective is to find a qualitative value, and define a decision point for mitigation purposes. In this case, this task is straightforward, just combining the impact and probability values. The final result appears in Table 2, where all elements with at least one High or greater value occurrence are considered. Analysing the table shows that counterfeit devices and Web applications are the resources considered most critical regarding security and on which further mitigation actions should be studied.

In this simple analysis, we deliberately ignore the important domino effect that results from exploiting one threat having an impact on another resources. This is the case of the Temporal Database, which, as it is not directly exposed to the Internet, shows a lower probability of attack success. However, attacks on Web applications will most certainly target this database (or even other components). The same rationale can be applied to fraudulent devices that could contaminate the same database. This is why we need to resort to more elaborate attack analysis techniques. However, in the first phase, this simple model helps better to contextualise information security with the most critical resources.

Table 2. Critical Asset/Impact and Threat success probability list.

Asset	Impact	Success Probability
Small programmable devices	**High**	**Very High**
Computer-like nodes	**High**	Low
Network nodes	**High**	Low
Temporal Database	**High**	**High**
Web applications	**High**	**Very High**

5   Conclusion

Cybersecurity is currently an essential management process that must be part of any ICT project from the start. This process is very complex, with Risk Assessment being one of its essential elements. In its application, in addition to recognising the security objectives of the project in question, a demanding reflection on threats and attacks is required. Several models have been applied in the most diverse projects, but no solution can be considered a winner. This paper describes an alternative method that uses the ATT&CK matrix to provide information about threats and attacks.

This method is applied to a project under development, Lab4USpaces, which aims to build a framework to support a Smart Campus. The application of the model proved to be quite effective, allowing the identification of the most critical resources and a qualitative estimate of the risks. However, it was also possible to identify some limitations. When consulting the ATT&CK matrix, some keywords extracted from the description of the project's architecture were used. The use of different terms naturally results in different outcomes, revealing uncertainty due to the absence of an adequate taxonomy, which needs further investigation.

On the other hand, it was decided to avoid a deeper analysis of attacks in identifying threats and for the sake of simplicity. This option aimed to streamline the process but hid cascading effects related to attacks that affect risk assessment results. When knowledge about threats is limited and in an early stage of development, the solution is quite helpful. However, it should be further developed in subsequent iterations of the risk management process. These issues will be further investigated in future work on the model.

References

1. CIS controls. https://www.cisecurity.org/controls
2. Miorandi, D., Sicari, S., De Pellegrini, F., Chlamtac, I.: Internet of things: vision, applications and research challenges. Ad Hoc Netw. **10**, 1497–1516 (2012). https://doi.org/10.1016/J.ADHOC.2012.02.016
3. Smart city standards - an overview (2017). https://urbanopus.net/smart-city-standards-an-overview/
4. Ahmed, M., Panda, S., Xenakis, C., Panaousis, E.: MITRE ATT&CK-driven cyber risk assessment, pp. 1–10. ACM (2022)
5. Al-Fuqaha, A., Guizani, M., Mohammadi, M., Aledhari, M., Ayyash, M.: Internet of things: a survey on enabling technologies, protocols, and applications. IEEE Commun. Surv. Tutorials **17**, 2347–2376 (2015). https://doi.org/10.1109/COMST.2015.2444095
6. Amro, A., Gkioulos, V., Katsikas, S.: Assessing cyber risk in cyber-physical systems using the ATT&CK framework. ACM Trans. Priv. Secur. **26**(2), 1–33 (2023). https://doi.org/10.1145/3571733
7. Anagnostopoulos, T., et al.: Challenges and solutions of surveillance systems in IoT-enabled smart campus: a survey. IEEE Access **9**, 131926–131954 (2021)
8. Atzori, L., Iera, A., Morabito, G.: The internet of things: a survey. Comput. Netw. **54**, 2787–2805 (2010). https://doi.org/10.1016/j.comnet.2010.05.010
9. Awang, N., Xanthan, A., Samy, L.N., Hassan, N.H.: A review on risk assessment using risk prediction technique in campus network. Int. J. Adv. Trends Comput. Sci. Eng. **9**(3) (2020)
10. Ayrour, Y., Raji, A., Nassar, M.: Modelling cyber-attacks: a survey study. Netw. Secur. **2018**(3), 13–19 (2018)
11. Babun, L., Denney, K., Celik, Z.B., McDaniel, P., Uluagac, A.S.: A survey on IoT platforms: communication, security, and privacy perspectives. Comput. Netw. **192**, 108040 (2021). https://doi.org/10.1016/j.comnet.2021.108040. scholar: 2 cit 4/2021
12. Strom, B.E., Applebaum, A., Miller, D.P., Nickels, K.C., Pennington, A.G., Thomas, C.B.: MITRE ATT&CK®: design and philosophy (2020). https://www.mitre.org/news-insights/publication/mitre-attck-design-and-philosophy
13. Brand, B.S., Rigo, S.J., Figueiredo, R.M., Barbosa, J.L.V.: Sapientia: a smart campus model to promote device and application flexibility. Adv. Comput. Intell. **2**, 18 (2022). https://doi.org/10.1007/s43674-022-00032-0
14. Chagnon-Lessard, N., et al.: Smart campuses: extensive review of the last decade of research and current challenges. IEEE Access **9**, 124200–124234 (2021). https://doi.org/10.1109/ACCESS.2021.3109516
15. Cisco: The internet of things reference model (2014). http://cdn.iotwf.com/resources/71/IoT_Reference_Model_White_Paper_June_4_2014.pdf
16. Elhayatmy, G., Dey, N., Ashour, A.S.: Internet of things based wireless body area network in healthcare. In: Dey, N., Hassanien, A.E., Bhatt, C., Ashour, A.S., Satapathy, S.C. (eds.) Internet of Things and Big Data Analytics Toward Next-Generation Intelligence. SBD, vol. 30, pp. 3–20. Springer, Cham (2018). https://doi.org/10.1007/978-3-319-60435-0_1
17. Elmaghraby, A.S., Losavio, M.M.: Cyber security challenges in smart cities: safety, security and privacy. J. Adv. Res. **5**, 491–497 (2014). https://doi.org/10.1016/j.jare.2014.02.006

18. Fielding, J.: Back to basics: tackling security threats in an increasingly complex world. Comput. Fraud Secur. **2019**, 6–8 (2019)
19. Friha, O., Ferrag, M.A., Shu, L., Maglaras, L., Wang, X.: Internet of things for the future of smart agriculture: a comprehensive survey of emerging technologies. IEEE/CAA J. Automatica Sinica **8**, 718–752 (2021)
20. Georgiadou, A., Mouzakitis, S., Askounis, D.: Assessing MITRE ATT&CK risk using a cyber-security culture framework. Sensors **21**(9), 3267 (2021). https://doi.org/10.3390/s21093267
21. Gomez, C., Chessa, S., Fleury, A., Roussos, G., Preuveneers, D.: Internet of things for enabling smart environments: a technology-centric perspective. J. Ambient Intell. Smart Environ. **11**, 23–43 (2019)
22. Haufe, K.: Maturity based approach for ISMS governance (2017)
23. He, T., Li, Z.: A model and method of information system security risk assessment based on MITRE ATT&CK. In: 2021 2nd International Conference on Electronics, Communications and Information Technology (CECIT). IEEE (2021). https://doi.org/10.1109/cecit53797.2021.00022
24. Hui, P.: Construction of information security risk assessment model in smart city. In: 2020 IEEE Conference on Telecommunications, Optics and Computer Science (TOCS). IEEE (2020). https://doi.org/10.1109/tocs50858.2020.9339614
25. Hussain, A.A., Bouachir, O., Al-Turjman, F., Aloqaily, M.: Notice of retraction: AI techniques for COVID-19. IEEE Access **8**, 128776–128795 (2020)
26. ISO/IEC: Iso/iec 27001:2013, information technology - security techniques - information security management systems - requirements (2013). https://www.iso.org/standard/54534.htmlhttps://www.iso.org/obp/ui/#iso:std:iso-iec:27001:ed-2:v1:en
27. ISO/IEC: Information technology-security techniques-information security management systems-overview and vocabulary (international standard ISO/IEC 27000) (2016). https://www.iso.org
28. Ivanov, D., Kalinin, M., Krundyshev, V., Orel, E.: Automatic security management of smart infrastructures using attack graph and risk analysis. In: 2020 Fourth World Conference on Smart Trends in Systems, Security and Sustainability (WorldS4). IEEE (2020). https://doi.org/10.1109/worlds450073.2020.9210410
29. Kalinin, M., Krundyshev, V., Zegzhda, P.: Cybersecurity risk assessment in smart city infrastructures. Machines **9**, 78 (2021). https://doi.org/10.3390/machines9040078
30. Kang, W., Deng, J., Zhu, P., Liu, X., Zhao, W., Hang, Z.: Multi-dimensional security risk assessment model based on three elements in the IoT system. In: 2020 IEEE/CIC International Conference on Communications in China (ICCC), pp. 518–523. IEEE (2020)
31. Kirimtat, A., Krejcar, O., Kertesz, A., Tasgetiren, M.F.: Future trends and current state of smart city concepts: a survey. IEEE Access **8**, 86448–86467 (2020)
32. Lea, R.: (2016). https://urbanopus.net/smart-city-standards-an-overview/
33. Liao, B., Ali, Y., Nazir, S., He, L., Khan, H.U.: Security analysis of IoT devices by using mobile computing: a systematic literature review. IEEE Access **8**, 120331–120350 (2020)
34. Min-Allah, N., Alrashed, S.: Smart campus-a sketch. Sustain. Cities Soc. **59**, 102231 (2020). https://doi.org/10.1016/j.scs.2020.102231. scholar: cit 95 4/2023
35. Miraz, M.H., Ali, M., Excell, P.S., Picking, R.: A review on internet of things (IoT), internet of everything (IoE) and internet of Nano things (IoNT). In: 2015

Internet Technologies and Applications, ITA 2015 - Proceedings of the 6th International Conference, pp. 219–224 (11 2015). https://doi.org/10.1109/ITECHA.2015. 7317398

36. NIST: SP 800-53 rev. 5 security and privacy controls for information systems and organizations (2020). https://csrc.nist.gov/publications/detail/sp/800-53/rev-5/ final

37. Oruc, A., Amro, A., Gkioulos, V.: Assessing cyber risks of an INS using the MITRE ATT&CK framework. Sensors **22**(22), 8745 (2022). https://doi.org/10. 3390/s22228745

38. Roy, S., Panaousis, E., Noakes, C., Laszka, A., Panda, S., Loukas, G.: SoK: the MITRE ATT&CK framework in research and practice (2023). https://doi.org/10. 48550/ARXIV.2304.07411

39. Santos, H.M.: Cybersecurity: A Practical Engineering Approach. CRC Press, Boca Raton (2022)

40. Stallings, W.: Effective Cybersecurity: A Guide to Using Best Practices and Standards. Addison-Wesley Professional, Boston (2018)

41. Tewari, A., Gupta, B.: Security, privacy and trust of different layers in internet-of-things (IoTs) framework. Future Gener. Comput. Syst. **108**, 909–920 (2020). https://doi.org/10.1016/j.future.2018.04.027

42. Vailshery, L.S.: IoT connected devices worldwide 2019–2030 (2022). https://www.statista.com/statistics/1183457/iot-connected-devices-worldwide/. Accessed 10 Apr 2023

43. Yassine, I., Halabi, T., Bellaiche, M.: security risk assessment methodologies in the internet of things: survey and taxonomy. In: 2021 IEEE 21st International Conference on Software Quality, Reliability and Security Companion (QRS-C), pp. 668–675. IEEE (2021)

44. Zahra, B.F., Abdelhamid, B.: Risk analysis in internet of things using EBIOS. In: 2017 IEEE 7th Annual Computing and Communication Workshop and Conference (CCWC), pp. 1–7. IEEE (2017)

45. Zammani, M., Razali, R., Singh, D.: Factors contributing to the success of information security management implementation. Int. J. Adv. Comput. Sci. Appl. (2019)

Privacy Concerns in Smart Indoor Environments in the Internet of Everything Era: A Smart University Campus Case Study

Andria Procopiou[1]($\boxtimes$) and Eliana Stavrou[2]

[1] Department of Computing, School of Sciences, University of Central Lancashire
Cyprus, Larnaca, Cyprus
`aprocopiou@uclan.ac.uk`
[2] Faculty of Pure and Applied Sciences, Open University of Cyprus, Nicosia, Cyprus
`eliana.stavrou@ouc.ac.cy`

Abstract. In the Internet of Everything era, indoor environment provides multiple benefits across different domains to their occupants such as improving their well-being and health, ensuring their safety, providing valuable assistance to their tasks and enhancing their experience using various types of intelligent sensors and devices. So far, we witnessed smart environments thriving in education, as they improve the overall experience, efficiency and education. One prominent example of is the smart university campus, empowered by IoE systems. Initially, such data is not considered sensitive, private and confidential to the occupants. However, through statistical analysis and machine learning, and in combination with heuristics and public information acquired, it can pose a significant risk to their privacy as it can directly leak personal information regarding their preferences, needs and interests. Unfortunately, the ICT systems of universities were targeted by numerous cyber attacks in the past. Therefore, it is only a matter of time before smart university campuses form the attack surface to novel privacy-leakage attacks. Hence, there is clear need for detailed and in-depth investigation. In this paper, we conduct a study on how the smart university campuses could leak sensitive information. We discuss how such information could threaten the occupants and their privacy, both in cyber and physical space, and the challenges related to their protection. Finally, we provide possible recommendations.

Keywords: Internet of Everything · Internet of Things · Smart Buildings · Smart Indoor Environments · Privacy · Security · Safety

1 Introduction

Technology forms a vital part of the society and the world, as of today. Various technologies such as smartphones, watches, thermostats, smart TVs, smart cars,

T. Pereira et al. (Eds.): IOECON 2023, LNICST 551, pp. 92–109, 2024.
https://doi.org/10.1007/978-3-031-51572-9_8

smart lighting systems and so on are becoming the norm, ultimately transforming our cities into smart intelligent entities of their own. This enhancement is mainly enabled by the Internet of Everything (IoE). IoE is denoted as a more holistic and complete set of technologies and concepts where computational devices, data, processes, AI and analytics come together with humans through the Internet for better decision-making, ultimately improving our lives [60].

IoT, a subset of IoE, denotes of all physical objects which have sensors and actuators embedded on them, have processing power, can be connected to the Internet and can communicate and directly exchange data with other similar entities without the need for a central authority through wireless communications [1,2]. IoT can be integrated into different types of indoor environments and transform them into smart entities of their own. Examples include residential homes, industrial and commercial buildings, stadiums, theatres, music venues, airports and universities, and schools.

IoT can also offer different types of services to the smart indoor environments and their occupants, such as providing assisted living, promoting sustainability and protecting the environment [5–7]. IoT sensors can monitor the indoor air and environment quality of the building, a vital part for the battle against Covid19. Furthermore, they can monitor the physical space and its occupants' behaviour and overall safety inside the building. They could also provide vital assistance and information to occupants with compromised health, special needs and/or disabilities. In certain smart buildings, the presence of smart appliances and devices in kitchens and dining areas can assist the occupants with their daily dietary and nutrition behaviour. Finally, the development of smart parking area spaces could help the occupants park their vehicles quickly and with minimum carbon emission and sound noise. Some examples of data collected through these services include room temperature, air quality, humidity, door locked/opened, visual presence, lights on/off, internal/external sounds, human motion and so on [6]. More information on the services smart indoor environments provide is presented in Sect. 2. Such data cannot be considered private, sensitive and confidential and directly related to the occupants.

Unfortunately, due to the IoT's weak security countermeasures, this data is relatively easy to be illegally obtained. The set of data compromised could indirectly reveal information and trends about the occupants' overall behaviour, interests, activities and preferences [3,4]. Using this data, the adversary can use machine learning and statistical analysis models to deduct private information of occupants as studies conducted [29,30] demonstrated.

More importantly, the illegally acquired data combined with heuristics, common knowledge, public timetables and building public information with regards to the smart indoor environment (e.g. wiring plans, floor plans) could possibly lead to the identification and possible profiling of individuals [6,9]. This could result in becoming a target in large-in-scale phishing campaigns or individual phishing campaigns. Furthermore, such an unfortunate scenario could threaten not only their privacy but also their physical safety.

Moreover, help of machine learning and statistical analysis models can deduct valuable information about the occupancy of spaces as studies conducted by

[29,30] showed. What is more concerning is that machine learning and statistical analysis in combination with heuristics, common sense, publicly available timetables social events and building-related public information can leak personal, private and sensitive information about the occupants.

In this paper, we conduct an in-depth investigation with regards to the privacy challenges in smart buildings, specifically smart university buildings, and the risk of its occupants private, sensitive and confidential information being revealed. Section 2 provides an introduction to the smart indoor environment definition and then focusing on the smart university campus and the different services it provides to its occupants. In Sect. 3, we present our case study with regards to smart university buildings and relevant privacy concerns that may arise from potential IoT-related data leakage. For every scenario considered, we present the impact that can have on individuals, their privacy and their safety. In Sect. 4, discuss on the impact caused on individual's privacy, consider possible challenges in ensuring privacy and briefly describe possible defence countermeasures, concluding that privacy is equally important as security. In the final section, we provide concluding remarks and what potential future work could be conducted.

2   Background Knowledge

2.1   Smart Indoor Environments

In general, any indoor environment is described as the indoor physical space that uses various technologies (e.g. IoT, analytics, artificial intelligence, the cloud, sensors/actuators and ubiquitous computing) to promote sustainability and protect the environment, provide assisted living to its occupants and enhance their experiences, ensure their safety and provide multiple services to them, monitor the indoor physical space and maintain its healthy state and ensure the availability of its services [5–7]. There are different categories of smart indoor environments depending on the services and type of occupants. Popular and notable types include but not limited to commercial and entertainment (e.g. shopping malls, stadiums, theatres, cinemas, music venues), corporate (e.g. companies and organisations), transportation (e.g. smart airports), health services (e.g. smart hospitals) and residential (e.g. smart homes). For the purpose of the study, we only consider a smart university campus.

2.2   Smart Services in Smart University Campuses

Indoor Air and Environment Monitoring: One of the most important benefits IoT technologies provided was the continuous monitoring of the indoor air quality. It has been the subject of numerous studies during the Covid19 era. Covid19 is transmitted through airborne particles and droplets. Infected individuals spread Covid19 by releasing particles and droplets contained in respiratory fluids into the air. Examples include breathing, speaking, singing, exercise, coughing and sneezing. The risk of being infected with Covid19 is significantly increased when people are in close proximity and indoors [19]. Furthermore, air quality monitoring was also a subject of interest beforehand due to people spending more time indoors than outdoors during the winter months [20,21].

Air pollutant levels can be built up much faster due to less frequent exchange of air [22]. Sensors should be placed in strategic locations, monitoring various air quality metrics such as dust fine particulate matter (PM), Ozone (O3), Carbon Monoxide and Dioxide, Nitrogen Dioxide [7]. Furthermore, other environmental metrics should be monitored such as temperature, humidity and sound to ensure the well-being of individuals [6]. The efficient monitoring of the indoor environment extends beyond the assessment of air quality. It is important for the smart university campus to provide thermal comfort as well as appropriate lighting and acoustic control to individuals for assisted living purposes [3,21].

Physical Space/Individuals Monitoring: Most universities are open and accessible to the public. Hence, it should be ensured that appropriate security and safety measures are deployed. In detail, proper access control sensors (e.g. intelligent door locks, token-based authentication systems, CCTV) are placed so students and staff members are properly authenticated and authorised and any irregular behaviour is quickly and accurately detected [7,23]. Furthermore, through similar sensors and technologies, real-time monitoring and tracking of individuals in smart university campuses is possible. Tracking services can assist towards the physical safety and security of individuals by immediately notifying security staff on the event of criminal acts. In addition, tracking services can assist in ensuring any Covid19 social distance measures are correctly followed [7,23]. Another important aspect is to regularly monitor the physical grounds of the university to detect any environmental abnormalities and prevent any natural disasters such as fires and floods. Sensors that are responsible for this functionality are fire, gas and flood sensors [24].

Health and Well-Being of Individuals Monitoring and Assistance: One important benefit of a smart university campus is that it can provide valuable assistance to students, staff and visitors with disabilities and other health problems [26]. It is essential that everyone feels safe, confident and included and not by any means restricted. Hence, the smart university campus should be accessible and usable to everyone regardless of any disabilities and/or health problems they might face and make their visit a pleasant one [18]. Firstly, the smart university campus should be able to consist of disabled access entrances, lifts, stairways, escalators and ramps in all the key orientation points to accommodate people with movement disabilities [10] as well as automatic door openings [13].

Secondly, the smart university campus should make relevant campus information and university services available in different video and/or audio formats. Furthermore, these information services should be able to make adjustments in their explanation provided to people with different abilities and needs. Specifically, dedicated sensors and technologies should be able to describe objects and places and help them navigate through them [11]. Finally, appropriate communication channels should be available to people so they can communicate with staff members in case they require additional help and assistance.

Moreover, any mobile smart medical equipment individuals carry with them (e.g. asthma inhalers, blood pressure monitors, blood glucose and diabetes monitors and other types of health and wellness trackers) should communicate with dedicated services of the smart university campus [17]. Through them, properly trained personnel can interfere and provide immediate help in case of a medical emergency [12]. We also have to note that all individuals exhibiting health problems and/or disabilities can carry a tracker sensor so the dedicated personnel can keep track of their movements inside the smart university campus and be ready to provide them immediate help without wasting any valuable time.

Finally, through the assistive environments the smart campus university offers the opportunity to its occupants to adjust a room's settings according to their needs and preferences. Examples include automated adjustment of lights, temperature and sounds to ease symptoms of anxiety, depression and other mental heath issues [3,12,14–16].

Smart Appliances/devices Monitoring: In dedicated kitchen facilities, which are most likely to only be accessed by staff members, there will be various smart appliances and devices available. Examples include smart fridges, microwaves, ovens, hobs, coffee machines and kettles [42]. These appliances will be able to assist individuals in their food and drink preparation [42]. Furthermore, staff members could potentially set up the dedicated fridges to inform them on possible food run-outs and could automatically place an order upon a run-out [43] through dedicated smart cameras and other sensors.

Smart Parking Services: University campuses, especially large ones in urban areas, consist of large parking spaces since not everyone is likely to live close to the university premises or able to use public transport to accommodate incoming drivers, cyclists and motorcyclists. A smart parking is bound to benefit the university staff, students and visitors, the environment as well as the ecosystem. The services deployed will be able to inform drivers, cyclists and motorcyclists on the parking availability and where it is located in the parking lots through, smart weight and measure sensors. Specifically, the weight and measure sensor at the entrance would check the incoming vehicle and guide the driver to the nearest available parking space [7]. In addition, special zones for emergency vehicles, loading vehicles and parking spaces for people with disabilities will be available as well as electric vehicle recharging points [7].

3 Smart University Buildings Privacy Concerns Case Study

In this section, we present the different use case scenarios where the privacy of individuals can be leaked using occupant and/or environment-related data from

Table 1. Privacy Leakage Scenarios Summary

Smart Service	Non-Private Data Acquired	Direct Private Data Leaked	Indirect Private Data Leaked
Air Qual	Indoor Pollut	Human Pres., Occupants No.	Role, Breaks, Locat., Sens. Info
Air Qual	Air Qual. Metr.	Human Pres., Occupants No.	Role, Breaks, Locat., Sens. Info
Air Qual	Temp./Humid	Human Pres., Occupants No.	Role, Breaks, Locat., Sens. Info
Phys. Space	Door Locks	Human Pres., Occupants No.	Durat., Entry/Exit, Breaks, Sleep ,Sens. Info
Phys. Space	Authen. Mechan	Human Pres., Occupants No.	Durat., Entry/Exit, Breaks, Sleep, Sens. Info
Phys. Space	CCTV log	Human Pres., Occupants No.	Durat., Entry/Exit, Breaks, Sleep, Sens. Info
Health	Heart rate	Heart Diseas. (e.g. arrhythmia)	Routes, Sens. Info
Health	Oxygen level	Respir. Diseas. (e.g. asthma, copd)	Routes, Sens. Info
Health	Blood Pres	Blood Pres. (hypertension 1, 2)	Routes, Sens. Info
Health	Disab. Ramps, Lifts Interact	Disab. Status	SRoutes, Sens. Info
Health	Help. Points Interact	Disab. Status	Routes, Sens. Info
Health	Lights Interact	Mental Healh Stat	Sens. Info
Health	Sounds Interact	Mental Healh Stat	Sens. Info
Health	Thermal Interact	Mental Healh Stat	Sens. Info
Smart Appl	Smart Appl. Data	Human Pres.	Durat., Breaks, Purpose, Sleep Patt., Sens. Info
Smart Parking	Vehicle weight, Dur., Model	Individ. Role, Disab. Stat	n/a

compromised IoT devices and sensors as well as accessible types of information, summarising them in Table 1. For space constraints reasons, we define sensitive data as the set of personal data to the individuals. This data includes age, gender, sexual orientation, marital status, medical and biological data, disability status, political views, interests and activities, religion, ethnic race, cultural background and financial information.

As highlighted in the paper so far, and previously argued by related studies [6], different types of IoT devices and sensors that collect environment-related data can reveal private-related information regarding the occupants, their movements and overall behaviour inside the environment and overall preferences [25].

As a result, adversaries can illegally acquire such data and use them for malicious purposes. The risk explained above in combination with other accessible types of information can lead to the identification and profiling of individuals [6,9], conduction of phishing campaigns and even threatening the physical safety of them. We define accessible types of information as the following:

– Heuristics and Common Sense: In a smart university campus, different types of occupants are likely to be located at the university's premises at different times. Examples include deducting that it is more likely that students will be present at the university late at night (e.g. studying, submitting coursework) and non-faculty members come before 7 am and leave no later than 5pm [9].
– Publicly available timetables and social events: Every university has a dedicated website which contains information regarding the faculty members and their expertise, the modules/course taught and even their calendars. It also contains publicly available information regarding the non-staff members, their

job roles within the university and where their offices are located. Furthermore, the website is likely to include information regarding the societies of the university currently established (e.g. description, meeting dates, boarding members) as well as events that are open to the public (e.g. open days) [9].

– Building-related public information: The university consists of multiple buildings. These buildings consist of wiring and floor plans as well as dedicated building information models. The buildings' classrooms, labs, lecture theatres and any room is likely to consist of a number and possibly a name if it is large enough. Therefore, every room in the university's buildings is likely to have dedicated sensors and devices which even if they cannot be accessed physically, their location can be revealed using building-related public information [9].

Indoor Air and Environment Monitoring Privacy Leakage Scenarios: The compromise of air quality monitoring sensors could reveal the presence of occupants inside a room and possibly for how long they stayed. Specifically, this can be achieved by monitoring the different levels of air quality metrics and indoor pollutants (e.g. Ozone, Carbon Monoxide, Carbon Dioxide, Air Velocity, Air Pressure) as well as other metrics such as indoor lights, temperature and humidity. [26, 27]. If there is someone present in the room, the lights are likely to be turned on and then turned off when they leave the room. The temperature could indicate the presence of occupants, and possibly the number of them. Humans live by breathing. Their respiration releases energy as heat and therefore, the room temperature will rise as occupants will release heat energy. Similarly, the carbon dioxide levels are elevated due to the occupants exhaling CO_2 [59]. Using this information, the adversary can work out how long the occupants stayed in a room(s), the possible route taken, possible entry/exit points and break sessions.

The illegally data acquired presented in combination with different types of accessible of information can in further reveal personal and sensitive information about the occupants of the smart university campus.

Combining the presence and number of occupants with heuristics and common sense data could reveal their role inside the university (e.g. student/academic staff member/non-academic staff member). It is more likely for students to be inside the smart university campus during the evening/late night hours and for non-academic staff members to be in early in the morning. In addition, if there are occupants located in different buildings of the smart university campus, the adversary could potentially work out if they had any social interactions or met in a common room.

Combining the presence and number of occupants with publicly available timetables, social events information and building-related public information can reveal personal information about the occupants' identity, interests and activities. Specifically, using names and room numbers and publicly acquired timetables the adversary could possibly find out about staff and non-staff members currently being at their office desks, specific students and staff members being in certain lectures theatres and/or labs at specific times. The academics' office room numbers are publicly available from the university website and the students' timetable could be relatively easily acquired from the university website. In addition, the smart university's societies and clubs tend to advertise their social events in the smart campus which is a public space and anyone can witness such information. Therefore, by combining human presence and this information, the adversary can make plausible assumptions about the individuals. For example, if the music society is hosting a concert, the adversary can deduct that the occupants are likely to be music students or have a strong interest in music.

Beyond the occupants' personal interests and activities, other more personal and sensitive information can be revealed. Examples include meetings of past alcoholics, victims of domestic violence, LGBT+ individuals, societies of various religions, faiths and ethnicity's, and cancer and other deadly diseases patients and survivors.

Physical Space/Individuals Monitoring Privacy Leakage Scenarios: The compromise of physical space and authentication mechanisms (intelligent door locks, token-based authentication systems) could initially reveal occupancy in rooms and number of occupants, provided that each occupants uses their personal token to enter a room. Every time an individual wants to enter a room using their personal token (e.g. campus card), the token-based authentication mechanism is activated upon and produces a signal. Therefore, the adversary will know if there is human presence in the room and possibly how many individuals are currently in the room.

Proceeding, the adversary can work out how long individuals stayed in a room, the entry/exit points they used and the possible route taken to enter a room. Furthermore, they could make plausible assumptions about the purpose of visit for example, if the card-authentication system of the library is activated, the individual (possibly a student) wants to enter the library.

In addition, other types of personal data can be revealed to the adversary such as sleep patterns. For example, if certain staff-members and/or students are more frequently present during the night it is possible their sleep patterns are shifted. Once again, similarly to the air quality data argument presented in the previous section, combining the presence and number of occupants with publicly available timetables, social events information and building-related public information can reveal personal information about the occupants' identity, interests and activities.

We also need to note that with the compromise of CCTV data, the identity of individuals can be revealed more accurately. This illegally acquired data in combination with the academic term timetables, the university's clubs and societies events timetables and other social events can give a more clear view of who exactly these individuals are. Bringing back the music society hosting a concert example, the adversary now has visual evidence of who these individuals are. Using image/video processing tools and software they can map specific individuals to their interests, activities and personal information. This can be proved particularly dangerous when it comes to sensitive data such as meetings of past alcoholics, victims of domestic violence, LGBT+ individuals, societies of various religions, faiths and ethnicity's, and cancer and other deadly diseases patients and survivors.

Health and Well-Being of Individuals Monitoring and Assistance Privacy Leakage Scenarios: Through the compromise of medical devices the occupants own (e.g. asthma inhalers, blood pressure monitors, blood glucose and diabetes monitors, fitness trackers), the adversary could obtain information about their health such heart rate, oxygen level, blood pressure and activity levels (step counting). Using this information, the adversary could work out on which potential diseases the individuals suffer from [8,17].

For example, if the medical device owner produces between an oxygen level rate between 88% and 92% oxygen they are likely to suffer from a mild chronic obstructive pulmonary disease [51]. On the other hand, an oxygen level of 97% or above indicates of a case of mild asthma, 92–97% indicates moderate asthma, and less than 92% is a strong indication of a severe asthma [56]. Another example consists monitoring the heartbeats of individuals. A pulse higher than 100 beats/second indicates tachycardia [52]. Statistically, it is more likely for women to have tachycardia than men as well as heavy smokers, people who have high blood pressure, diabetes and people suffering from anxiety [52].

In addition, by monitoring the blood pressure, the adversary can work out if the patient is suffering from various blood pressure conditions such as elevated blood pressure, hypertension stage or hypertension stage 2. In elevated blood pressure, readings consistently range between 120–129 systolic and less than 80 mm Hg diastolic. In hypertension stage 1, readings consistently range from 130–139 systolic or 80–89 mm Hg diastolic. Finally, in hypertension stage 2, readings range at 140/90 mm Hg or higher [53]. Using these simple rules, the adversary could assume from what kind of hypertension disease the individual suffers from. Moreover, the adversary could use simple statistics to determine other sensitive information about the individuals such as age, gender, family medical history and ethnic race. In detail, the probability of having blood pressure problems increases with age. With regards to gender, men before the age of 55 have a higher probability of demonstrating blood pressure problems while women after menopause. Blood pressure problems also tend to run in families. Finally, it is statistically observed that African Americans are at increased risk for showing blood pressure issues [53].

Furthermore, the adversaries could learn more about an occupant's disability status by monitoring the interactions of an individual with the dedicated spaces. For example, if an individual has used the dedicated disabled ramps and/or lifts, then the adversary will know that the said individual exhibits mobility problems.

On the other hand, through the occupants' interaction with the dedicated IoT sensors and devices offering information in different formats (e.g. video, audio, alternative explanations), the adversary can obtain information about the occupants' abilities and needs such as occupants exhibiting visual, auditory impairments or being neurodivergent (e.g. autism, adhd). Specifically, an individual with visual impairment will choose to interact with auditory information and an individual with auditory impairment will choose to interact with visual information. Individuals who are classified as neurodivergent could choose to be presented with information in alternative formats according to their needs.

Regarding individuals exhibiting different health problems and/or disabilities, their overall movement inside the smart university campus can be acquired as they could carry a tracker sensor with them to gain immediate help from personnel in case of emergency.

In addition, through compromising a room's visual and acoustic settings based on occupants' personal preferences and needs, the adversary could make plausible assumptions regarding their mental health and well-being [45]. People who suffer seasonal affective disorder, depression and sleep disorders may choose specific light settings (e.g. light therapy lamps) to ease their symptoms [54]. According to [46], visual comfort at work is directly related to the occupants' performance, after-work hours as well as sleep quality.

Another impact aspect is that through the room's thermal acoustic settings, gender, age and possible metabolic rates could be plausibly assumed. Older people are more likely to get cold easily and women have lower metabolic rates than men [47–49]. Finally, through the acoustic settings of a room, the adversary could make assumptions about the individuals' anxiety levels as binaural beats have been used to ease anxiety [55].

Smart Appliances/devices Monitoring Privacy Leakage Scenarios: Illegally smart appliances/devices monitoring acquired data can immediately reveal human presence, as an individual directly interacts with them. Using the acquired data, the adversary can work out the dietary customs of individuals for example, the adversary can work out when and how often individuals drink coffee/tea by monitoring their interactions with the smart coffee/tea machine. Another example would include on when the individuals are having lunch/dinner/snack by monitoring their interactions with the smart oven/microwave/fridge. In addition, by working out the specific timestamps of the interactions, the adversary could learn more about the individuals' sleep patterns. For example, if an individual regularly interacts with the smart appliances during the night, it is possible they sleep during the day. Using the same timestamps, the adversary could work out how long the individuals stayed in the kitchen and if they had any interactions with each other, depending on the duration they stayed in. Finally, by compromising the cameras and sensors inside the smart fridge, the adversary could gain information about their food preferences, possible allergies and diseases the occupants might have and store chains preferences.

Smart Parking Services Privacy Leakage Scenarios: Illegally smart parking services data acquired could reveal private information on the occupants' vehicle. Specifically, through compromising the dedicated weight sensors, the vehicle's model could be leaked as each vehicle has its own specific weight [7]. In addition, based on the parking space the vehicle is parked, the adversary could deduct on whether the vehicle is an emergency, loading, disabled-assistive or electric. Furthermore, if the smart university campus consists of dedicated parking areas based on the driver's role at the university, the driver's university role could be leaked. In addition, using the weight sensors, the adversary can possibly work out how long the driver has stayed in.

4   Discussion, Challenges and Possible Countermeasures

4.1   Discussion on Privacy Leakage Impact

Undoubtedly, privacy should be of equal focus to security in a smart university campus since, as presented in this paper, the risk of privacy leakage of individuals even through non-personal data is exceptionally high [8,28]. The fact that IoT devices and sensors are not able to accommodate sophisticated and complex security countermeasure due to lack of hardware resources makes their compromise a relatively easy and straightforward task [8].

Furthermore, as also demonstrated in the paper, simple yet valuable assumptions based on the information gained about individuals can lead to successful phishing campaigns. The adversary can use all the private, sensitive and personal information gathered to either target specific people (most likely in key positions) within the university in a spear phishing attack.

A spear phishing example could target individual people such as the rector of a university. The rector is likely to have their own dedicated parking space (if they drive a vehicle). After gaining the necessary information about their vehicle model, the adversary could send a phishing email with regards to their vehicle such as service is needed and they need to provide their credit card information to authorise the payment. Since a rector's personal details (e.g. name, profession) is likely to be listed in the university's website, the adversary could make the phishing email more personal (e.g. personal greeting) and therefore more believable to the victim. Another example would consist of a person high in status inside the university (e.g. head of the department, dean, head of finance, HR manager). These people are likely to have their own offices with smart appliances facilities (e.g. smart fridge, smart coffee machine) for their own usage. A spear phishing attack would consist of the food chain the individual buys food/coffee from informing them that they need to re-enter their credit card bank details otherwise their order will not be placed.

On the other hand, the adversary could target large groups of people in general phishing campaigns. An example could consist of the adversary targeting students with disabilities to sign up for extra assistive services by giving personal information about them such as date of birth, gender, telephone number, address and additional information regarding their disability status. Another example would consist of all the students to re-register for the new academic year in their course due to a "system malfunction". On the event of a successfully completing a phishing campaign (either general or spear type), the adversary could use the newly acquired personal information to threaten the individuals in further in multiple ways both in physical and cyber space. In detail, the adversary could:

- Physically threaten the individual's physical safety provided that they acquire their corresponding address. Examples could include the adversaries illegally entering their house to perform an act of burglary or threaten the individual and/or their family, stalking the individuals or vandalising the victim's residential premises.
- Perform malicious acts of social engineering to illegally obtain more sensitive information about the victim. Using personal information already obtained through the compromise of the IoT sensors and/or a successful phishing campaign, the adversary could deceive the victim in further. This could happen by disguising themselves as a familiar service the victim uses. Examples include, the adversary pretending to be a bank staff member, calling to "confirm the victim's personal information" or "re-authorising a payment due to a malfunction". Credit card details could be obtained from a successful phishing campaign. Another example would consist of the adversary disguising themselves as a staff member from the food chain the victim shops groceries from to "confirm the victim's personal and bank details for an order placed". Such data could be obtained from compromising the victim's food and its associated data placed in the smart fridge.
- Blackmail individuals through extortion in exchange of not revealing sensitive information about them. Examples could include extortionists threatening individuals with exposing data about their sexual orientation, gender identification, religion, ethnic race, cultural background, political views, health and genetics and financial data.
- Steal an individual's identity. Since the adversary acquired a plethora of different personal information about the victim, they can illegally authenticate themselves as the victim to gain access to other services the victim has. An example would be to "regain access to a bank account after losing the card" by answering relevant security questions. If the security questions have to do with acquired information the adversary has (e.g. mother's maiden name, favourite sports team, first car, city grew up, university attended) they can easily bypass them and gain access to the account so they can deposit funds to their own.

4.2 Challenges in Ensuring Privacy

IoT networks, such as the smart university campus, comes with its own set of network and device requirements. An IoT network includes a massive number of IoT sensors and devices [57] that can be deployed with a considerable distance to each other. Specifically, it is estimated that a typical a smart IoT environment contains 1000 s of devices [58]. We also have to consider that in a smart university campus, there is a great chance of a dynamic number of IoT devices entering and leaving the network. In addition, these devices can also be mobile (e.g. medical devices) [36]. Unarguably, a large-scale network produces an even greater traffic size that takes more time to properly monitor for malicious behaviour. In addition, the mobility and the dynamic nature of the IoT devices connected to the network is challenging, as they can join and leave the network from anywhere in the smart university campus. Therefore, it is easier for them to bring external threats right to the network. An IoT device entering the network may already be compromised and cause further issues to the network such as trying to spread malware and then exit the network immediately to avoid detection.

Another important issue to consider is that each IoT device comes with its own set of protocols, standards and functionality [36]. Many of the IoT devices use non IP-based protocols and other IoT-based protocols such as CoAP, MQTT, XMPP, AMQP and so on. Each of them have their own headers, commands and payload sizes. Therefore, the traffic generated is heterogeneous, and it could be potentially harder to monitor as it is more difficult to define a distinct baseline of what traffic is considered legitimate and which is considered malicious.

Furthermore, we should address that IoT devices and sensors are low in resources, specifically memory, processing power and storage. Therefore, they are unable to accommodate any sophisticated and complex security counter-measures [8] such as intrusion detection systems, robust authentication protocols and complex encryption schemes. As a result, adversaries can easily compromise a large number of them and acquire a plethora of different data to expose the individuals' privacy as demonstrated in this paper.

Moreover, we should highlight that confidentiality is not equivalent to privacy [31]. Confidentiality is defined as cyber security principle that ensures that information is protected from unauthorised disclosure. In practice, data and information either stored or exchanged between users remains secure from eaves-droppers through the usage of appropriate encryption techniques. However, this does not guarantee that the privacy of the data will remain intact. Privacy (in cyberspace) gives the freedom to users to control their own personal information. Hence, even if users' data is encrypted, it could still be shared with third-parties and other organisations due to insufficient security policies in place [50]. Not all users are familiar with appropriately handling the access rights to their data. Therefore, misconfigurations can occur without the user's knowledge.

4.3   Possible Countermeasures to Ensure Privacy

Encryption might not fully guarantee the privacy of individuals but it certainly ensures confidentiality, where the information and data exchanged between different nodes is encrypted and secure. However, sophisticated and complex encryption can cause a computational overhead which is unacceptable to IoT devices and senors from a resources perspective [8,41]. Therefore, there is need for lightweight encryption schemes which are potentially equally accurate as their more complex equivalents. Exceptional proposed systems have been proposed so far however, more work needs to be conducted [32–35]. Proceeding, the deploy-ment of zero-knowledge proofs could be a strong solution towards ensuring the privacy of the occupants. Zero-knowledge proofs denote the techniques which the cloud server can verify a response to a query sent by a device without actually seeing the data. Previous work involving smart meter data [37] demonstrated reassuring results. Since data is significantly related to the privacy issues in our case, defence countermeasures that are directly related to data will pose a set of effective solutions. One popular solution is data obfuscation, where the data is substantially modified by adding noise to the data. In that way, statistical analysis is made harder to be successfully conducted. Previous work conducted in [38] demonstrated that data obfuscation can defend against occupancy detection using smart meter data.

Another important solution is the anonymisation of data. Anonymisation is where the data is significantly changed so the identity of individuals is hard to be leaked. Appropriate anonymisation techniques could be integrated on data so no indication about the occupants' lives is leaked [39,40]. Furthermore, another suggestion would be to keep the data stored locally and not sent to any third parties and/or cloud servers. If the data is stored locally, it cannot be compromised through any communication channel attacks and therefore, the attack vectors are decreased [3]. In addition, even if the data is not directly related to the occupant, appropriate security policies could be introduced for each individual. In that way, the occupants will be able to have a clear view of the security policies in place and will have more control of the data generated from their interaction with the smart university campus and its services [3].

5   Future Work and Concluding Remarks

In this paper, we performed an in-depth investigation of the privacy concerns a smart university campus could pose to its occupants. We highlighted that data collected from the environment and interactions with the university's occupants could eventually reveal personal and confidential information about the occupants even though are not directly related to them cannot be classified as private on its own. This could have serious consequences to the privacy of individuals, from leakage of sensitive information to profiling of them, to successful phishing campaigns, stealing their identities and even their lives being threatened. Hence, it is essential that appropriate handling of such data is conducted through the effective deployment of privacy enhancing technologies. In terms of future work, we aim to practically evaluate our assumptions with regards to the privacy risk posed on individuals in smart university campuses by deploying the appropriate IoT technologies and ultimately investigating and developing appropriate privacy enhancing solutions.

References

1. Mattern, F., Floerkemeier, C.: From the internet of computers to the internet of things. In: Sachs, K., Petrov, I., Guerrero, P. (eds.) From Active Data Management to Event-Based Systems and More. LNCS, vol. 6462, pp. 242–259. Springer, Heidelberg (2010). https://doi.org/10.1007/978-3-642-17226-7_15

2. Procopiou, A., Chen, T.M.: Security challenges and solutions in IoT networks for the smart cities. In: Internet of Things, 1st edn., pp. 161–204. CRC Press, Boca Raton (2022)
3. Chen, D., Bovornkeeratiroj, P., Irwin, D., Shenoy, P.: Private memoirs of IoT devices: safeguarding user privacy in the IoT era. In: 2018 IEEE 38th International Conference on Distributed Computing Systems (ICDCS), pp. 1327–1336 (2018). https://doi.org/10.1109/ICDCS.2018.00133
4. Weinberg, B.D., Milne, G.R., Andonova, Y.G., Hajjat, F.M.: Internet of things: convenience vs. privacy and secrecy. Bus. Horizons 58(6), 615–624 (2015). https://doi.org/10.1016/j.bushor.2015.06.005
5. Perera, C., Zaslavsky, A., Christen, P., Georgakopoulos, D.: Sensing as a service model for smart cities supported by internet of things. Trans. Emerg. Telecommun. Technol. 25(1), 81–93 (2014)
6. Mace, J.C., Morisset, C., Pierce, K., Gamble, C., Maple, C., Fitzgerald, J.: A multi-modelling based approach to assessing the security of smart buildings. In: Living in the Internet of Things: Cybersecurity of the IoT - 2018, pp. 1–10 (2018). https://doi.org/10.1049/cp.2018.0031
7. Righetti, F., Vallati, C., Anastasi, G.: IoT Applications in Smart Cities: A Perspective Into Social and Ethical Issues. In: 2018 IEEE International Conference on Smart Computing (SMARTCOMP), pp. 387–392 (2018). https://doi.org/10.1109/SMARTCOMP.2018.00034
8. Alami, A., Benhlima, L., Bah, S.: An overview of privacy preserving techniques in smart home wireless sensor networks. In: 2015 10th International Conference on Intelligent Systems: Theories and Applications (SITA), pp. 1–4 (2015). https://doi.org/10.1109/SITA.2015.7358409
9. Pappachan, P., et al.: Towards privacy-aware smart buildings: capturing, communicating, and enforcing privacy policies and preferences. In: 2017 IEEE 37th International Conference on Distributed Computing Systems Workshops (ICDCSW), pp. 193–198 (2017). https://doi.org/10.1109/ICDCSW.2017.52
10. Kalikova, J., Krcal, J., Sterba, M.: Use of iBeacon technology for safe movement of disabled people. In: 2021 Smart City Symposium Prague (SCSP) (2021). https://doi.org/10.1109/SCSP52043.2021.9447392
11. Orza, O., Constantin, F., Negoita, A., Bosoc, S.C., Balaceanu, C., Suciu, G.: Indoor air quality monitoring for improvement of the environment in smart toilets. In: 2021 16th International Conference on Engineering of Modern Electric Systems (EMES), pp. 1–4 (2021). https://doi.org/10.1109/EMES52337.2021.9484146
12. Marques, G., Pitarma, R.: An indoor monitoring system for ambient assisted living based on internet of things architecture. Int. J. Environ. Res. Public Health 13(11), 1152 (2016)
13. Lymperopoulos, P., Meade, K.: PathPass: opening doors for people with disabilities. In: 2014 4th International Conference on Wireless Mobile Communication and Healthcare - Transforming Healthcare Through Innovations in Mobile and Wireless Technologies (MOBIHEALTH), pp. 32–35 (2014). https://doi.org/10.1109/MOBIHEALTH.2014.7015902
14. McColl, S.L., Veitch, J.A.: Full-spectrum fluorescent lighting: a review of its effects on physiology and health. Psychol. Med. 31(6), 949–964 (2001)
15. Rejeh, N., Heravi-Karimooi, M., Tadrisi, S.D., Jahani, A., Vaismoradi, M., Jordan, S.: The impact of listening to pleasant natural sounds on anxiety and physiologic parameters in patients undergoing coronary angiography: A pragmatic quasi-randomized-controlled trial. Complement. Therap. Clin. Pract. 25, 42–51 (2016). https://doi.org/10.1016/j.ctcp.2016.08.001. ISSN 1744-3881

16. Ashkenazy, T., Einat, H., Kronfeld-Schor, N.: Effects of bright light treatment on depression- and anxiety-like behaviors of diurnal rodents maintained on a short daylight schedule. Behav. Brain Res. **201**(2), 343–346 (2009). https://doi.org/10.1016/j.bbr.2009.03.005. ISSN 0166-4328
17. Keshavarz, M., Anwar, M.: Towards improving privacy control for smart homes: a privacy decision framework. In: 2018 16th Annual Conference on Privacy, Security and Trust (PST), pp. 1–3 (2018). https://doi.org/10.1109/PST.2018.8514198
18. Salha, R.A., Jawabrah, M.Q., Badawy, U.I., Jarada, A., Alastal, A.I.: Towards smart, sustainable, accessible and inclusive city for persons with disability by taking into account checklists tools. J. Geogr. Inf. Syst. **12**(04), 348–371 (2020)
19. Chao, C.: Transport phenomena of human exhaled droplets due to respiratory action in ventilated indoor environments. Hong Kong Med. J. **14**(5 Suppl), 19–22 (2008)
20. Raysoni, A.U., Stock, T.H., Sarnat, J.A., et al.: Characterization of traffic-related air pollutant metrics at four schools in El Paso, Texas, USA: implications for exposure assessment and siting schools in urban areas. Atmos. Environ. **80**, 140–151 (2013)
21. Saini, J., Dutta, M., Marques, G.: A comprehensive review on indoor air quality monitoring systems for enhanced public health. Sustain. Environ. Res. **30**(1), 1–12 (2020)
22. Rawi, N.A.M.N., Jalaludin, J., Chua, P.C.: Indoor air quality and respiratory health among Malay preschool children in Selangor. Biomed. Res. Int. **2015**, 248178 (2015)
23. Gupta, D., Bhatt, S., Gupta, M., Tosun, A.S.: Future smart connected communities to fight COVID-19 outbreak. Internet Things **13**(100342), 100342 (2021)
24. Ramapatruni, S., Narayanan, S.N., Mittal, S., Joshi, A., Joshi, K.: Anomaly detection models for smart home security. In: 2019 IEEE 5th Intl Conference on Big Data Security on Cloud (BigDataSecurity), IEEE Intl Conference on High Performance and Smart Computing, (HPSC) and IEEE Intl Conference on Intelligent Data and Security (IDS), pp. 19–24 (2019). https://doi.org/10.1109/BigDataSecurity-HPSC-IDS.2019.00015
25. Mace, J.C., Morisset, C., Smith, L.: A socio-technical ethical process for managing access to smart building data. In: Living in the Internet of Things (IoT 2019) (2019). https://doi.org/10.1049/cp.2019.0135
26. Zhang, W., Wu, Y., Calautit, J.K.: A review on occupancy prediction through machine learning for enhancing energy efficiency, air quality and thermal comfort in the built environment. Renew. Sustain. Energy Rev. **167**(112704), 112704 (2022)
27. Bakó-Biró, Z., Wargocki, P., Weschler, C.J., Fanger, P.O.: Effects of pollution from personal computers on perceived air quality, SBS symptoms and productivity in offices. Indoor Air **14**(3), 178–187 (2004)
28. Bugeja, J., Jacobsson, A., Davidsson, P.: On privacy and security challenges in smart connected homes. In: 2016 European Intelligence and Security Informatics Conference (EISIC), pp. 172–175 (2016). https://doi.org/10.1109/EISIC.2016.044
29. Jin, M., Bekiaris-Liberis, N., Weekly, K., Spanos, C., Bayen, A.: Sensing by proxy: occupancy detection based on indoor CO2 concentration. Berkeley.edu (2015)
30. Jin, M., Bekiaris-Liberis, N., Weekly, K., Spanos, C.J., Bayen, A.M.: Occupancy detection via environmental sensing. IEEE Trans. Autom. Sci. Eng. **15**(2), 443–455 (2018). https://doi.org/10.1109/TASE.2016.2619720
31. Jin, R., He, X., Dai, H.: On the security-privacy tradeoff in collaborative security: a quantitative information flow game perspective. IEEE Trans. Inf. Forensics Secur. **14**(12), 3273–3286 (2019). https://doi.org/10.1109/TIFS.2019.2914358

32. Khashan, O.A.: Hybrid lightweight proxy re-encryption scheme for secure fog-to-things environment. IEEE Access **8**, 66878–66887 (2020). https://doi.org/10.1109/ACCESS.2020.298431

33. Roy, S., Rawat, U., Karjee, J.: A lightweight cellular automata based encryption technique for IoT applications. IEEE Access **7**, 39782–39793 (2019). https://doi.org/10.1109/ACCESS.2019.2906326

34. Fotovvat, A., Rahman, G.M.E., Vedaei, S.S., Wahid, K.A.: Comparative performance analysis of lightweight cryptography algorithms for IoT sensor nodes. IEEE Internet Things J. **8**(10), 8279–8290 (2021). https://doi.org/10.1109/JIOT.2020.3044526

35. Camtepe, S., et al.: Compcrypt-lightweight ANS-based compression and encryption. IEEE Trans. Inf. Forensics Secur. **16**, 3859–3873 (2021). https://doi.org/10.1109/TIFS.2021.3096026

36. Gubbi, J., Buyya, R., Marusic, S., Palaniswami, M.: Internet of things (IoT): a vision, architectural elements, and future directions. Future Gener. Comput. Syst. **29**(7), 1645–1660 (2013)

37. Molina-Markham, A., Danezis, G., Fu, K., Shenoy, P., Irwin, D.: Designing privacy-preserving smart meters with low-cost microcontrollers. In: Keromytis, A.D. (ed.) FC 2012. LNCS, vol. 7397, pp. 239–253. Springer, Heidelberg (2012). https://doi.org/10.1007/978-3-642-32946-3_18

38. Chen, D., Irwin, D., Shenoy, P., Albrecht, J.: Combined heat and privacy: preventing occupancy detection from smart meters. In: 2014 IEEE International Conference on Pervasive Computing and Communications (PerCom), pp. 208–215 (2014). https://doi.org/10.1109/PerCom.2014.6813962

39. Bordel, B., Alcarria, R., Robles, T., Iglesias, M.S.: Data authentication and anonymization in IoT scenarios and future 5G networks using chaotic digital watermarking. IEEE Access **9**, 22378–22398 (2021). https://doi.org/10.1109/ACCESS.2021.3055771

40. Attaullah, H., et al.: Fuzzy-logic-based privacy-aware dynamic release of IoT-enabled healthcare data. IEEE Internet Things J. **9**(6), 4411–4420 (2022). https://doi.org/10.1109/JIOT.2021.3103939

41. Ghali, C., Tsudik, G., Wood, C.A.: When encryption is not enough: privacy attacks in content-centric networking. In: Proceedings of the 4th ACM Conference on Information-Centric Networking (2017)

42. Ständer, M., Hadjakos, A., Lochschmidt, N., Klos, C., Renner, B., Mühlhäuser, M.: A Smart Kitchen Infrastructure. In: 2012 IEEE International Symposium on Multimedia, pp. 96–99 (2012). https://doi.org/10.1109/ISM.2012.27

43. Edward, M., Karyono, K., Meidia, H.: Smart fridge design using NodeMCU and home server based on Raspberry Pi 3. In: 2017 4th International Conference on New Media Studies (CONMEDIA), pp. 148–151 (2017). https://doi.org/10.1109/CONMEDIA.2017.8266047

44. Ukil, A., Bandyopadhyay, S., Pal, A.: IoT-privacy: to be private or not to be private. In: 2014 IEEE Conference on Computer Communications Workshops (INFOCOM WKSHPS), pp. 123–124 (2014). https://doi.org/10.1109/INFCOMW.2014.6849186

45. Serghides, D.K., Chatzinikola, C.K., Katafygiotou, M.C.: Comparative studies of the occupants' behaviour in a university building during winter and summer time. Int. J. Sustain. Energy **34**(8), 528–551 (2015)

46. Chang, C.Y., Chen, P.-K.: Human response to window views and indoor plants in the workplace. HortScience **40**(5), 1354–1359 (2005)

47. Katafygiotou, M.C., Serghides, D.K.: Bioclimatic chart analysis in three climate zones in Cyprus. Indoor Built Environ. **24**(6), 746–760 (2015)
48. Nicol, J.F., Humphreys, M.A.: Adaptive thermal comfort and sustainable thermal standards for buildings. Energy Build. **34**(6), 563–572 (2002)
49. Smolander, J.: Effect of cold exposure on older humans. Int. J. Sports Med. **23**(2), 86–92 (2002)
50. Stavrou, E.: Guidelines to develop consumers cyber resilience capabilities in The IoE ecosystem. In: Pereira, T., Impagliazzo, J., Santos, H. (eds.) IoECon 2022. LNICST, vol. 458, pp. 18–28. Springer, Cham (2022). https://doi.org/10.1007/978-3-031-25222-8_2
51. NICE. Quality statement 6: Emergency oxygen during an exacerbation, Chronic obstructive pulmonary disease in adults Quality standards (2011)
52. Tachycardia. Cleveland Clinic. https://my.clevelandclinic.org/health/diseases/22108-tachycardia. Accessed 03 Sept 2022
53. High blood pressure and older adults. National Institute on Aging. https://www.nia.nih.gov/health/high-blood-pressure-and-older-adults. Accessed 03 Sept 2022
54. Terman, M., Terman, J.S.: Light therapy. Health Prog. **4**(3), 5 (1998)
55. Binaural beats are being used as sound wave therapy for anxiety, but does it really help? Prevention (2021). https://www.prevention.com/health/mental-health/a35782370/binaural-beats-for-anxiety/. Accessed 03 Sept 2022
56. Asthma workup. Medscape.com (2022). https://emedicine.medscape.com/article/296301-workup. Accessed 03 Sept 2022
57. Abdul-Qawy, A.S., Pramod, P., Magesh, E., Srinivasulu, T.: The internet of things (IoT): an overview. Int. J. Eng. Res. Appl. **1**(5), 71–82 (2015)
58. Pekar, A., Mocnej, J., Seah, W.K.G., Zolotova, I.: Application domain-based overview of IoT network traffic characteristics. ACM Comput. Surv. **53**(4), 1–33 (2021). https://doi.org/10.1145/3399669. Article 87
59. Carbon dioxide in indoor air. Ncceh.ca. https://ncceh.ca/documents/field-inquiry/carbon-dioxide-indoor-air. Accessed 03 Sept 2022
60. Kiesler, N., Impagliazzo, J.: Perspectives on the internet of everything. In: Pereira, T., Impagliazzo, J., Santos, H. (eds.) IoECon 2022. LNICST, vol. 458, pp. 3–17. Springer, Cham (2023). https://doi.org/10.1007/978-3-031-25222-8_1

People-to-People (P2P)

Curricular Excursions on the Internet of Everything

John Impagliazzo[1]([envelope]) [ORCID], Natalie Kiesler[2] [ORCID], and Juan Chen[3] [ORCID]

[1] Hofstra University, Hempstead, NY, USA
john.impagliazzo@hofstra.edu
[2] DIPF Leibniz Institute for Research and Information in Education,
Frankfurt am Main, Germany
kiesler@dipf.de
[3] National University of Defense Technology, Changsha, Hunan, China
juanchen@nudt.edu.cn

Abstract. Including dispositions and skills in computing curricula is beginning to take root in education circles. These two dimensions complement the knowledge dimension to form an understanding of competency taken in context. In a parallel movement, the Internet of Everything (IoE) is an emerging area of learning that focuses on the interaction between people and machines (things) involving data and processes on the internet. It is time, therefore, to channel student studies toward a competency-based IoE curriculum. This work attempts to initiate a discussion on this goal by proposing a "Draft 0" curriculum on the IoE that reflects competency, where students prepare to enter the workplace upon graduation. The proposed curriculum intends to stimulate discussion and garner more significant insight into developing a competency-based study plan on the Internet of Everything.

Keywords: Internet of Everything · IoE · computing education · computing curricula

1 Introduction

Dispositions, skills, and knowledge taken in context form the three competency components. Recent curricula recommendations, like the IT2017 [21] and CC2020 [1] reports, highlight the importance of transitioning from a knowledge-based educational setting to competency-based education. In addition, global industries and businesses seek computing and engineering graduates that are adaptable, collaborative, inventive, meticulous, passionate, proactive, professional, purpose-driven, responsible, responsive, and self-directed [9]. These eleven defined competency dispositions appear in the CC2020 report. Table 1 describes a listing containing the meaning of these dispositions.

Studies have shown that dispositions are necessary for a successful career [3]. It would seem unimaginable to think that industrial and governmental institu-

T. Pereira et al. (Eds.): IOECON 2023, LNICST 551, pp. 113–125, 2024.
https://doi.org/10.1007/978-3-031-51572-9_9

Table 1. CC2020 Dispositions

Disposition	Elaboration
Adaptable	Flexible; agile, adjust in response to change
Collaborative	Team player, willing to work with others
Inventive	Exploratory, look beyond simple solutions
Meticulous	Attentive to detail; thoroughness, accurate
Passionate	Conviction, strong commitment, compelling
Proactive	With initiative, self-starter, independent
Professional	Professionalism, discretion, ethics, astute
Purpose-driven	Goal-driven, achieve goals, business acumen
Responsible	Use judgment, discretion, act appropriately
Responsive	Respectful; react quickly and positively
Self-directed	Self-motivated, determination, independent

tions would only accept a graduate with some of these eleven attributes. Therefore, computing and engineering educational programs should address dispositions fully in their teaching, learning, and assessing approaches. Doing so could help their placement practices. Since only 5% of graduates continue to graduate school [17], 95% of the graduates of such programs must possess these eleven elements in various levels of achievement as they enter the workplace.

In this work-in-progress paper, the authors examine current industry expectations toward graduates who seek to apply for the Internet of Everything (IoE) or related positions. The goal is to begin a conversation by proposing an IoE curriculum and associated competencies that could benefit learners seeking the equivalent of an IoE specialty or degree. It also explores the IoE implications for computing education.

The IoE area is relatively new, starting about a dozen years ago. The 2023 IoECon website describes the Internet of Everything as follows.

The internet of everything has four essential components: things, people, data, and processes. Things consist of machines, devices, and sensors that form the fundamental objects of the IoE ecosystem. People provide the intellectual basis of the IoE since humans analyze data and create essential insights from operations. Data form another IoE component, whose content increases each year exponentially and whose management becomes increasingly complex. Process is the fourth IoE component that determines how each of the other three elements provides increased digital value by transferring data to the right person or device [4].

In short, the IoE may be defined as "a distributed network of connections between people, smart things, processes, and data, whereas these components interact and exchange real-time data" [10].

As with all new fields, it is difficult to recommend what students must learn and know, and how to perform in the workplace. However, describing a study plan for IoE in the context of competency only provides a first step in achieving study recommendations for the emerging discipline.

Given this description, indicating some information related to IoT education is beneficial. As with other areas of computing and engineering, a community of educators emerges to address how community members can participate in improving the entity at hand. This community often establishes organizations and related conferences to promote community attributes and debate challenges. In addition, such entities often have curricular recommendations for topic or course enhancement and even recommended degree programs. The authors present a "Draft0" for a possible curriculum for the Internet of Everything.

The objectives of this work-in-progress are to (a) develop a minimal curriculum for IoE students seeking an undergraduate degree, (b) identify which competency elements might accompany curricular recommendations, and (c) describe what computing and engineering educators can do to promote competency in an undergraduate IoE curriculum. This preliminary study builds on methods already used in professional disciplines and describes some principles to attract competent IoE graduates into industry and government.

2   Background

The ACM/IEEE Computing Curricula 2020 (CC2020) report recommended that university programs focus on competency-based learning instead of knowledge-based learning. This approach changes the way computing educators should teach and evaluate students. From the IT2017 and the CC2020 reports, professional competency from an academic perspective is:

$$Competency = Knowledge + Skills + Dispositions$$

in the context of performing a task. However, this same concept, from an industry perspective, would likely take this form:

$$Competency = Dispositions + Skills + Knowledge$$

in the context of performing a task. Although equivalent to the first version, this second version emphasizes dispositions and skills, followed by knowledge.

Having the proper dispositions and skills means the person hired fits into the workplace with the expected characteristics and must then be able to perform on the job with little attention to the person's knowledge background. Therefore, having the requisite knowledge to support dispositions and skills becomes an advantage in the workplace. Hence, this study will emphasize a "performance first" approach for an IoE curriculum.

The emergence of the Internet of Everything with the elements of competency in computing education suggests competency in IoE studies. Competency is essential to IoE education because an IoE student and graduate should be able to "fit" into the workplace. Such a graduate should have a diverse background with skills needed for people-to-people (P2P), people-to-machine (P2M), and machine-to-machine (M2M) data processes over the internet. Educators should remember this when developing courses and programs related to the Internet of Everything. Figure 1 shows an image of competency within a professional or IoE context.

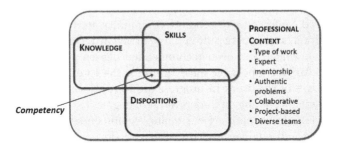

Fig. 1. Visualization of competency from the IT2017 report

From an educational viewpoint, educators have specialized in the knowledge domain of computing and engineering for many decades. However, teachers have also considered student skills over centuries and millennia. For example, becoming an artist or a craftsperson required the tutelage of established artisans who transferred skills to their students. However, they likely needed to pay more attention to their trade's dispositional and knowledge dimensions. This is unfortunate because, then and now, employers have had a keen interest in hiring people with proper behaviors and some knowledge in addition to the skills students might have. Dispositions reflect the workplace behaviors of a competent individual; knowledge is what an individual knows. Therefore, prospective employers would likely hire a graduate who had demonstrated all or most of the eleven dispositions in addition to skills and knowledge. Promoting dispositions in computing education is, however, still subject to research [5,7,11,13,15,22]. The same applies to teaching and assessing dispositions.

It would be beneficial to highlight a few developments to motivate the reason for fostering competency as a broad need for computing and engineering in IoE settings. Some of the earliest work on computing competencies emerged in software engineering. In 2011, Mead and Shoemaker [16] described the software assurance (SwA) competency model comprising knowledge, skills, and effectiveness. As before, the knowledge dimension is what an individual knows, skills are what an individual can do by applying knowledge, and effectiveness is the ability to utilize knowledge and skills productively. In simpler terms, effectiveness reflects behavior attributes, i.e., dispositions, such as being adaptable, meticulous, or purpose-driven.

The first computing curricular report to include dispositions explicitly was Information Technology 2017 (IT2017), defining competency as the combination of knowledge, skills, and dispositions in context [21]. Dispositions, described as "socio-emotional skills, behaviors, and attitudes that characterize the inclination to carry out tasks and the sensitivity to know when and how to engage in those tasks" [18], were not explicitly listed in IT2017 as they were assumed to be exhaustive and self-evident in human behavior. Subsequent curricular reports such as Information Systems 2020 (IS2020) [14] and Data Science 2021 (DS2021) [2] also embraced competency as a basis for computing education.

3   Curricular Structure and Fundamentals

For an Internet of Everything curriculum structure, first assume a traditional baccalaureate four-year student experience where each year partitions into two semesters. This assumption is common. However, a baccalaureate degree program can vary from three to six years in some locales worldwide.

3.1   Credit Structure

Typically, the four-year arrangement contains 120 semester hours or credits in the U.S. In Europe, a baccalaureate program typically has 180 or 210 points within the European Credit Transfer System (ECTS), earned within six or seven semesters. This translates to 30 credits or 60 ECTS for each full year of an academic program.

Again, the concept of a semester hour or credit can vary worldwide. In the United States, one semester hour or one credit equals 750 min of classroom study. Within the four years of study, the equivalent of one year is often dedicated to general studies and education, such as philosophy and history. The match of another year usually encompasses mathematics, science, and related subjects. What remains are two years of study or the equivalent of 60 credits (semester hours). In China, a university's requirements for a bachelor's degree are typically 120 credits, similar to the requirements in the United States. These credits often include general education credits and the specific technical, mathematics, and science requirements for a degree.

In Europe, one ECTS credit point equals 30 h of student work, including in-class time, self-study or group work, and projects. On average, a European university would award 5 ECTS credits per course. However, it is also possible to award 2, 3, 6, or 8 ECTS for a course. Typically, a university would have six courses per semester, two semesters yearly. Hence, a student typically should achieve 30 ECTS per semester, which equals 900 h of work, the equivalent of a full-time job.

3.2   Mathematics, Science, and General Education

Before delving into IoE subjects in a degree program, it is worthwhile to address some non-IoE areas. Firstly, one year of general studies often reflects the vision and mission of the university or institution. In that sense, such studies are beyond the scope of this work. This curriculum component might also include current elements of diversity, equity, inclusion, and accessibility [8]. Secondly, the year (equivalent to 30 credits or 60 ECTS) of mathematics and science is essential for IoE students since they must be competent in their work and make decisions supported by scientific methods and quantitative and qualitative analysis. Hence, approximately 50% of the curriculum should encompass non-IoE studies, leaving about 60 credits, or 90 to 105 ECTS, for IoE studies. In this paper, we provide credit point suggestions for the U.S. system with suggested ECTS units.

The mathematics and natural science component should encompass the subject areas in support of IoE learning and workplace performance. The 30 credits (semester hours) should include the following areas with credits described in parentheses.

- Discrete Mathematics (3 credits or 6 ECTS)
- Applied Probability and Statistics (6 credits or 12 ECTS)
- Calculus for Business (3 credits or 6 ECTS)
- Quantitative Analysis (3 credits or 6 ECTS)
- Qualitative Analysis (3 credits or 6 ECTS)
- Science with Laboratory (Biology, Chemistry, Physics) (6 credits or 12 ECTS)
- Mathematics/Science Electives (6 credits or 12 ECTS)

The course titles and assigned credits will vary depending on an institution's mission. For example, science courses may have four or more credits each because of content depth and laboratory time.

IoE students need an understanding of discrete mathematics because they require a knowledge of computing machines that operate in discrete rather than continuous modes. Probability and statistics are essential for IoE students because many computing decisions rely on numerical data to form good executions. Calculus is necessary for problem-solving strategies related to applications. IoE students focus on people-to-people and people-to-machine approaches in enterprise environments. Hence, knowing mathematics for business applications is essential for a competent IoE graduate. Analyzing strategic problems may involve quantitative and qualitative methods to extract information from (big) datasets. The techniques needed for exploring such issues will require different strategies. Hence, students should be aware of the two paradigms to address these modes of analysis.

Natural science should be part of an IoE education. The reason is the scientific method used in related subject areas. Because machines/things are part of an IoE paradigm, the scientific learning method is a meaningful way to approach IoE problems. As a suggestion, some form of classical physics would be an adequate choice to address the machine-to-machine or people-to-machine problem-solving strategies. Chemistry or biology could also work but less effectively than physics. Even so, approximately one year of the IoE curriculum constitutes the mathematics and science component.

The fundamental subject areas in mathematics and science should support competency foundations to enhance workplace performance, as already stated. It would also be interesting to attain more information and research to consolidate the integration of mathematics and natural science in IoE learning. However, it is too early to determine why the recommended courses would not satisfy a curriculum to produce a competent graduate.

4 Internet of Everything Curriculum Background

It is not the intention to specify precise IoE subject areas for an IoE curriculum. Instead, the intent is to propose general curricular areas to foster discussion and increased study for a meaningful curriculum. The broad curricular areas must involve the internet with processes and data that include P2P, P2M, and M2M. For simplicity, one can assume commutativity for people-to-machine. That is, people-to-machines and machines-to-people (P2M and M2P) are equivalent to this discussion.

Furthermore, the machine-to-machine aspect of IoE correlates with the Internet of Things (IoT) phenomenon that has emerged over the past quarter century. This term first appeared in 1999 and referred to any machine or thing with a binary (off-on) switch connected to the internet [6]. IoT programs have emerged worldwide, especially in China, where the subject leads to undergraduate and graduate degrees [23]. For perspective purposes, Appendix A shows a four-year IoT curriculum at the Florida International University (FIU). The curriculum at this institution forms an IoT exemplar in shaping a model curriculum for the Internet of Everything.

As mentioned, the general education degree component and the mathematics/science degree component are approximately thirty credits each. Therefore, for a four-year degree involving 120 credits, the IoE component should be about 60 credits. One could partition these credits into required foundation (core) courses, required advanced technical studies, elective technical courses, and free electives. For convenience, one can assume that all courses are three credits each. Therefore, the plan is to develop up to twenty IoE courses for the program. Again for convenience, assume approximately six foundation courses (18 credits), eight required advanced technical courses (24 credits), four elective technical courses (12 credits), and two free elective courses (6 credits). Two of the required advanced technical courses should be significant team projects related to IoE to address the disposition component of competency.

5 Internet of Everything Subject Categories

A breakdown of this plan follows. The course codes are arbitrary and used only for identification. The course names intend to provide meaning in the IoE domain and accentuate the "knowledge" dimension of competency. The "skills" and "dispositions" dimensions are suggestions to fulfill the extent of competency in producing a competent graduate by graduation. The two-course project should exploit all skills and all dispositions of the student. Also, parallel computing is relevant everywhere now, so exposure to parallel computing should be part of all IoE curricula.

5.1   Foundation Category

The Foundation Category comprises approximately six courses or 18 credits. This category should provide the basis for most other IoE activities. The student experiences or courses in this category generally occur within the first two years of study. For example, these courses might be the following.

IOE101 Introduction to the Internet of Everything
IOE102 Computers and Society
IOE103 Introduction to Python Programming
IOE104 Introduction to Web Programming
IOE201 Computer Organization
IOE202 Network Fundamentals and Security

The structure of the Foundation Category suggests new thinking and is adaptable based on the institution's mission. Each course should focus on student performance, where students practice related skills in their learning. The specific skills conveyed to students depend on the institution.

At this level, students become aware of the dispositions or attributes expected in the workplace. For example, teachers could promote collaboration with programming pairs or teams or require the meticulous application of network fundamentals. The early development of dispositions and skills, in addition to knowing content, is a positive first step in producing a competent graduate in the discipline.

5.2   Advance Category

The Advance Category comprises eight courses or 24 credits. This category of courses must build on the experiences developed in the Foundation Category. These student experiences generally occur in a four-year program's second and third years of study. The suggested courses are as follows.

IOE203 Elements of Data Structures
IOE204 Introduction to Data Science
IOE301 User Experience
IOE302 Data and Data Analytics
IOE303 Parallel and Distributed Processing
IOE304 Database Systems
IOE305 Social Informatics Operating Systems
IOE306 Internet of Everything Networking

As with the foundation courses, this category should suggest new thinking and is adaptable based on the institution's mission. Again, the focus should be on student performance, where students continue to develop skill sets coupled with the continued awareness of the dispositions expected in the workplace. Educators should foster as many of the dispositions shown in Table 1. The goal is to develop competent IoE graduates with the right attitude (dispositions) and the necessary skills to perform successfully in the workplace. In addition, teachers should enhance the people-to-people, the people-to-machine, and the machine-to-machine paradigms when offering courses in the Advance Category.

5.3   Electives Category

The Elective Category consists of four courses or 12 credits selected from a list of experiences related to the IoE. The following suggested courses often occur in the last year of study. However, students may also choose them with the intent of some IoE specialization. The following list is a suggestion. Institutions should offer electives based on their needs and mission.

IOE401 Computing Ethics
IOE402 Machine Learning
IOE403 Internet of Everything Project Management
IOE404 Internet of Everything Application Security
IOE405 Cloud Computing
IOE406 Embedded Systems for IoE
IOE407 Principles of Cybersecurity
IOE408 IoE Sensors and Controllers
IOE409 Software Strategies for IoE
IOE410 Wireless Protocols
IOE411 Internet of Everything Entrepreneurship
IOE412 System Design and Implementation
IOE413 Operating Systems
IOE414 Advanced Topics on the Internet of Everything
IOE415 Internet of Everything Systems
IOE416 Strategies for High-Performance Computing

As with the Advance Category, educators should enhance the P2P, P2M, and M2M paradigms in elective courses. Again, promoting and assessing dispositions and skills is essential for these student experiences [8,12].

5.4   Project Category

The Project Category comprises two courses or 6 credits. This category should be the most important of all the categories. Students should focus on a challenging project and dig deep into learning and skill development. All eleven dispositions should be active, and a complement of skills should emerge in developing competency and demonstrating performance.

IOE491 Major Project 1
IOE492 Major Project 2

All projects should be highly structured with an IoE focus (e.g., P2P, M2P, or M2M). This finishing computing experience should focus on the knowledge, skills, and dispositions acquired in earlier coursework. The project should incorporate proper computing standards (e.g., IEEE and ISO standards) and multiple realistic constraints (e.g., security, welfare, social, and economic factors). In addition to educators, people from business and industry should assist in evaluating all significant projects.

5.5 Free Category

The Free Category consists of two courses or six credits. This category suggests that students should be able to learn additional topics on the Internet of Everything or explore new areas of learning such as music, art, or business. In addition, all students should be free to discover areas of their interest, contributing to holistic personal development upon graduation [19,20].

6 Conclusions and Future Work

This effort is a work in progress as a first step in establishing a curriculum for the Internet of Everything. This competency-based approach (knowledge, skills, and dispositions) ensures that IoE graduates are ready for the workplace. The IoE curricular structure followed a four-year pattern. However, other ways are also possible based on geographic region and custom. In all cases, an equivalent of at least two years or 60 credits encompasses the technical portion of an IoE curriculum.

Establishing a new curriculum is complex and will face several challenges, e.g., resistance to change, lack of resources, and the need to prepare educators respectively. Most people have yet to discover the Internet of Everything and IoE education and will need time to develop. One of the first challenges is understanding what IoE is. This same challenge affected the Internet of Things in its early days, but now most people understand IoT and curricula exist for this branch of computing. Another challenge is the establishment of an IoE community of educators. That community would begin to emerge as IoE and IoE education proliferates in college and university courses and eventually in IoE curricula and degree programs. Time will tell how IoE will progress. First, however, presenting some basic ideas about IoE and IoE education is essential.

This work still needs time for completion. The intention is that this first step will encourage researchers to generate new perspectives and discussions on an IoE curriculum. Furthermore, since IoE is a superset of IoT, an IoT curriculum should only be part of an IoE curriculum. In addition to a things-to-things (T2T) paradigm, IoE must address the people-to-things P2T) and the people-to-people (P2P) paradigms. Hence, the Internet of Everything could open new doors and ideas encompassing various computing competencies. Thus, IoE represents a new dimension in computing education.

Acknowledgments. The authors wish to acknowledge the European Alliance for Innovation (EAI) for supporting the Internet of Everything (IoE) conferences, and this work.

Appendix A

FLORIDA INTERNATIONAL UNIVERSITY (FIU)

INTERNET OF THINGS TECHNICAL CURRICULUM

https://internetofthings.fiu.edu/courses/

Core Courses
CGS 2518 Data Analysis (3)
CGS 3767 Computer Operating Systems (3)
CDA 3104 Introduction to Computer Design (3)
CEN 3721 Introduction to Human-Computer Interaction (3)
COP 2250 Programming in Java (3)
CTS 1120 Fundamentals of Cybersecurity (3)
CNT 3122 Sensors for IoT (3)
CNT 3142 Microcontrollers for IoT (3)
CNT 3162 Intro. to Wireless Communications for IoT (3)
CNT 4165 Network Protocols for IoT (3)
EGN 2271 Introduction to Circuits and Electronics (3)
EEL 2880 Applied Software Techniques in Engineering (3)
EEL 4730 Programming Embedded Systems (3)
EEL 4734 Embedded Operating Systems (3)
EEE 4717 Introduction to Security of IoT and Cyber-Physical Systems (3)
TCN 2720 Intro to IOT (2)
TCN 4211 Telecommunications Networks (3)
TCN 4940 Senior Project (3)

Electives

Network Forensics & Securitys
TCN 4081 Telecommunication Network Security (3) (Prereq: TCN 4211)
TCN 4212 Telecommunication Network Analysis and Design (Prereq: TCN 4211)
TCN 4431 Principles Network Mngmt & Control Standards (Prereq: TCN 4211)
IoT Privacy (New Course, Prereq: EEL 2880)
Wireless Protocols for IoT (New Course, Prereq: TCN 4211)
IoT Forensics (New Course, Prereq: Embedded Programming for IoT)

Cyber Security
EEL 4806 Ethical Hacking & Countermeasures (Prereq: EEL 2880)
EEL 4802 Intro. Digital Forensics Eng. (Prereq: EEL 4806)
EEL 4804 Intro. Malware Reverse Eng. (Prereq: EEL 4806)

Data System Software
MAD 2104 Discrete Mathematics
COP 2210 Programming I

COP 3337 Programming II (Prereq: COP 2250 or COP 2210 or EEL 2880)
COP 3530 Data Structures (Prereq: COP 3337 and MAD 2104)
COP 4338 Computer Programming III (Prereq: COP 3350)
COP 4604 Unix Programming (Prereq: COP 4338, Coreq: COP 4610)
COP 4610 Operating Systems Principles (Prereq: COP 4338)

Entrepreneurship
EEL 4933 Engineering Entrepreneurship
EEL 4062 Engineering Business Plan Development
EEL 4351 Intro to Business Decisions.

References

1. CC2020 Task Force: Computing curricula 2020 (CC2020): Paradigms for future computing curricula. Technical report, Association for Computing Machinery, IEEE Computer Society, New York, NY, USA (2020). https://www.acm.org/binaries/content/assets/education/curricula-recommendations/cc2020.pdf
2. Danyluk, A., Leidig, P.: Computing competencies for undergraduate data science curricula. Technical report, Association for Computing Machinery, New York, NY, USA (2021). https://www.acm.org/binaries/content/assets/education/curricula-recommendations/dstf_ccdsc2021.pdf
3. Dede, C., Etemadi, A.: Why dispositions matter for the workforce in turbulent, uncertain times (2021). https://projects.iq.harvard.edu/files/nextlevellab/files/nll_brief_2._dispositions.july_2021.pdf
4. European Alliance for Innovation: EAI internet of everything conference (IOE-CON) (2023). https://ioecon.eai-conferences.org/2023/
5. Impagliazzo, J., Kiesler, N., Kumar, A.N., Mackellar, B., Raj, R.K., Sabin, M.: Perspectives on dispositions in computing competencies. In: Proceedings of the 27th ACM Conference on on Innovation and Technology in Computer Science Education, ITiCSE 2022, vol. 2, pp. 662–663. ACM, New York (2022). https://doi.org/10.1145/3502717.3532121
6. Foote, K.D.: A brief history of the internet of things (2022). https://www.dataversity.net/brief-history-internet-things/
7. Kiesler, N.: On programming competence and its classification. In: Proceedings of the 20th Koli Calling International Conference on Computing Education Research, Koli Calling 2020. Association for Computing Machinery, New York (2020). https://doi.org/10.1145/3428029.3428030
8. Kiesler, N., Impagliazzo, J.: Implementing diversity, equity, and inclusion in accreditation. In: 2022 International Symposium on Accreditation of Engineering and Computing Education (ICACIT). pp. 1–6 (2022). https://doi.org/10.1109/ICACIT56139.2022.10041468
9. Kiesler, N., Impagliazzo, J.: Industry's expectations of graduate dispositions. In: 2023 IEEE Frontiers in Education Conference (FIE), pp. 1–5 (2023)
10. Kiesler, N., Impagliazzo, J.: Perspectives on the internet of everything. In: Pereira, T., Impagliazzo, J., Santos, H. (eds.) IoECon 2022. LNICST, vol. 458, pp. 3–17. Springer, Cham (2023). https://doi.org/10.1007/978-3-031-25222-8_1

11. Kiesler, N., et al.: Computing students' understanding of dispositions: a qualitative study. In: Proceedings of the 2023 Conference on Innovation and Technology in Computer Science Education, ITiCSE 2023, vol. 1, pp. 103–109. ACM, New York (2023). https://doi.org/10.1145/3587102.3588797

12. Kiesler, N., Thorbrügge, C.: Socially responsible programming in computing education and expectations in the profession. In: Proceedings of the 2023 Conference on Innovation and Technology in Computer Science Education, ITiCSE 2023, vol. 1, pp. 443–449. Association for Computing Machinery, New York (2023). https://doi.org/10.1145/3587102.3588839

13. Kumar, A.N., et al.: Quantitative results from a study of professional dispositions. In: Proceedings of the 54th ACM Technical Symposium on Computer Science Education, SIGCSE 2023. ACM, New York (2023). https://doi.org/10.1145/3545947.3576335

14. Leidig, P., et al.: CIS 2020. A competency model for undergraduate programs in information systems. Technical report. ACM, New York (2020). https://is2020.hosting2.acm.org/2021/06/01/is2020-final-draft-released/

15. MacKellar, B.K., Kiesler, N., Raj, R.K., Sabin, M., McCauley, R., Kumar, A.N.: Promoting the dispositional dimension of competency in undergraduate computing programs. In: 2023 ASEE Annual Conference & Exposition. ASEE Conferences (2023). https://peer.asee.org/43018

16. Mead, N.R., Shoemaker, D.: The software assurance competency model: a roadmap to enhance individual professional capability. In: 2013 26th International Conference on Software Engineering Education and Training (CSEE&T), CSEE&T 2013 (2013). https://doi.org/10.1109/CSEET.2013.6595243

17. Murphy, T.J.: How many people go to graduate school and a few other questions (2017). https://blog.gradschoolmatch.com/people-going-graduate-school/

18. Perkins, D.N., Jay, E., Tishman, S.: Beyond abilities: a dispositional theory of thinking. Merrill-Palmer Q. **39**(1), 1–21 (1993). https://www.jstor.org/stable/23087298

19. Raj, R., et al.: Professional competencies in computing education: pedagogies and assessment. In: Proceedings of the 2021 Working Group Reports on Innovation and Technology in Computer Science Education, ITiCSE-WGR 2021, pp. 133–161. ACM, New York (2021). https://doi.org/10.1145/3502870.3506570

20. Raj, R.K., et al.: Toward practical computing competencies. In: Proceedings of the 26th ACM Conference on Innovation and Technology in Computer Science Education, ITiCSE 2021, vol. 2, pp. 603–604. Association for Computing Machinery, New York (2021). https://doi.org/10.1145/3456565.3461442

21. Sabin, M., et al.: Information technology curricula 2017 (IT2017). Technical report. ACM/IEEE Computer Society, New York (2017)

22. Sabin, M., et al.: Fostering dispositions and engaging computing educators. In: Proceedings of the 54th ACM Technical Symposium on Computer Science Education, SIGCSE 2023, vol. 2. ACM, New York (2023). https://doi.org/10.1145/3545947.3569592

23. Zhang, M., Zhang, L.: Undergraduate it education in China. ACM Inroads **5**(3), 49–55 (1993). https://doi.org/10.1145/2655759.2655774

Planning of Urban Freight Delivery During Peak and Off-Peak Traffic Periods

Olesia Hriekova[1,2,3](✉) (iD), Andrii Galkin[1,4] (iD), Tibor Schlosser[2] (iD),
Oleksii Prasolenko[1], and Nadiia Sokolova[1]

[1] Beketov National University of Urban Economy in Kharkiv, 17 Marshala Bazhanova Street,
O.M, Kharkiv 61002, Ukraine
`olesia.hriekova@kname.edu.ua`
[2] Slovak Technical University in Bratislava, Bratislava 81107, Slovakia
[3] University of Rome Tor Vergata, 00133 Rome, Italy
[4] University of Antwerpen, 2000 Antwerp, Belgium

Abstract. Paper present influence of time windows during the day on efficiency of urban freight delivery. Field research was obtained to gathering freight logistics data according to which models were build. The regression models obtained in the paper described the speed of delivery in the network during peak and off-peak periods and allow one to evaluate parameters of the freight tours process in the current scenario. Obtaining the choice of time periods has an impact on delivery tours: load capacity of a vehicle, quantity of delivery bays, etc. The results are useful for logistics operators, planners, and authorities.

Keywords: Urban · Regression analysis · Time Period · Delivery · emission

1 Introduction

The main feature of the modern development of cities is application of management approaches and methods that would allow the creation of the most comfortable living conditions for the population. It is this content that is included in the concept of sustainable development of the city from the point of view of its economic, ecological and social development. As of today, the sustainable development of transport in cities is mostly considered in terms of the development of population mobility, while the solution of issues of rational organisation of freight traffic is usually given little attention. But for the sustainable development of the city, the freight transport subsystem is no less important, since the success of forming a comfortable urban environment also depends on the quality of its functioning.

The constantly growing number of residents in cities leads to an increase in the demand for freight transportation. As a result, the number of freight vehicles on urban roads is increasing. This, in turn, becomes one of the reasons for the occurrence of traffic jams on the roads, which is reflected in the delivery time of all categories of users of the city's transport system and road safety in general.

Published by Springer Nature Switzerland AG 2024. All Rights Reserved
T. Pereira et al. (Eds.): IOECON 2023, LNICST 551, pp. 126–138, 2024.
https://doi.org/10.1007/978-3-031-51572-9_10

Furthermore, freight transport has the greatest negative impact on the environment [1, 2]. According to the UN Commission for the Sustainable Development of Settlements, the share of global greenhouse gas emissions from the operation of heavy vehicles is 22% [3]. In cities, this indicator is significantly higher due to the concentration of a large number of mobile sources of pollution in the space defined by the city boundary. On the basis of this, it can be stated that the issue of rational organisation and planning of the work of freight transport under the conditions of sustainable development of the city is an urgent task and requires research.

Recently Information and Communication Technologies (ICT), as well as the Intelligent Transport Systems (ITS) have become more popular. It supports planners and, stakeholders in general, to make the supply-chain processes more sustainable and effective. Various approaches are being developed to introduce innovative technologies into Urban Freight Transport. This allows planners to assess the situation in real time and organise the delivery taking into account the criteria used by stakeholders.

The field of the emerging technologies becomes larger and more popular.

It is possible to identify Internet of Things (IoT) that impact directly on city logistics toward a smart city logistics. In fact, in recent years, the evolution of emerging information and communication technologies (e-ICT) has opened the road to develop and implement new integrated and dynamic City Logistics solutions, allowing to improve the level and the quality of life of city users (e.g., residents, visitors). In particular, telematics can support the effectiveness of each action that can be implemented in light of the sustainability and liveability of the urban area.

IoT technology can be applied to consider the purchase of goods as information, for example, providing their availability in retailers' locations. It can also be used to forecast future end-consumer demand and flow of goods. It is useful to manage the routes in real-time and solve a Vehicle Route Problem (VRP) in advance.

2 References Review

2.1 Urban Freight and Sustainability

The physical distribution of goods carried out by freight transport in cities is the result of meeting the needs of the population, production, and construction in freight transportation. Under the conditions of high competition in the market of transport services, motor companies strive to satisfy as many requests for freight transportation as possible to maximise their profits, not disdaining various methods to successfully perform this task. As a result, the city receives an irrational loading of the transport network, and, as a result, residents are dissatisfied with the operation of the transport system [4].

To ensure the right of the urban population to a high standard of living in conditions of economic and environmental security, local self-government bodies in close cooperation with specialists in the field of transport must consider and solve the issue of optimising the city's transport system in a comprehensive manner, considering all its components, including the freight transportation subsystem.

Today, urban logistics is being researched from different sides. Due to the increase in the number of goods and their movement, there is a problem for urban logistics. Different researchers investigate this issue and identify the main areas of influence of the rapid development of goods movement in the city. There are such main problems of urban logistics: urban growth, traffic congestion and environmental problems. When they are combined, similar effects appear, such as the disruption of the urban delivery network, which is not found in the literature on developing countries. It must be said that some government agencies have adopted sustainable initiatives. They focused on distribution operations such as optimizing transport networks and logistics facilities, managing fleet size, improving facility regulation, routing, night delivery, and integer delivery systems (e.g. crowdshipping, parcel lockers). These innovative solutions, which have been successfully adopted in some countries, can be evaluated for possible implementation in other countries [5].

Many scientists are working on Green logistics issues to reduce the costs of logistic and pollution simultaneously. Many solutions are connected to new advanced green vehicles, the technology of their operations, etc. Otherwise, the network effect will have a system with a different set delivery time during the day. Given the following conditions, it is necessary to take research different scenarios of distribution during the day (peak; off-peak) was conducted to understand the behaviour of all networks to efficiency of each scenario. Thus, in some countries, time windows of distribution have been introduced, which limit the access of heavy vehicles to the city centre or determine the time period for the distribution of goods. Each city determines its own time periods for peak and off-peak deliveries [6, 7]. Due to this, Cattaruzza D. et al. consider time windows as optimisation of vehicle routes in urban logistics [8]. On the part of the government, this restriction refers to the limited access to certain special areas during certain periods.

Taniguchi, Thompson and Yamada [9] highlight the challenges of urban freight delivery during peak and off-peak periods, including congestion, environmental impacts, and safety concerns. A range of solutions to address these challenges, including the use of alternative delivery methods, such as bike and electric vehicle delivery, and the implementation of intelligent transportation systems were discussed to sustainable delivery [10]. The Holguín-Veras et al. [11] discuss the potential benefits of off-peak delivery, such as reduced congestion and improved environmental performance. Cidell and Regan [12] discuss range of strategies, including off-peak deliveries, consolidation of shipments, and use of alternative delivery methods, can be effective in reducing congestion, emissions, and other negative impacts on urban environments. However, presented works are been short in presenting direct numerical influence of peak and off-peak periods on the urban freight delivery parameters (e.g. time, speed, load factor, length of the route, etc.)

2.2 Methods of Estimating Vehicle Speed in Urban Area

The speed of the transport flow is directly influenced by the delivery time. Many factors affect this setting. Based on the work [13], experimental data from the Greenshields Linear Speed-Concentration Model can be used. Various methods can be used to determine the speed of the transport flows. In general, all methods can be divided into field and modelling methods [14–18]. The method of field research consists in obtaining actual speed values in the given space and during the specified period. This method consists in conducting direct observations.

Vehicle speed estimation can be carried out by modelling methods [19, 20]. The advantages of on-site monitoring of the speed of delivery are their greater accuracy, ease of use. The disadvantages are the high labour capacity and material cost of conducting the examinations, especially when special technical means and vehicles are used. The use of this group of methods is possible at the stage of collecting the necessary statistical information. For example, when developing models of transport flows. The second group of methods for estimating vehicle speed involves the use of models of transport flows. To establish communication between various pairs of basic characteristics of transport flow can be used: experimental data [21] and built on them functions, conclusions made during the analysis of boundary conditions, physical analogues.

At this time several approaches have been developed to estimate the speed of delivery in the conditions of urban transport networks [22]. The functioning of transport systems of large cities is largely estimated by the attributes of transport networks. Among all parameters of transport processes, the most important place belongs to speed delivery and same time of vehicles by the transport network. As indicators, which characterize the level of development of the transport network, one can accept the density of the transport network and the level of the automobile. Therefore, the average speed of delivery depends on the density of the transport network and level of automobilization [22–24]. According to this method, when the network density is increased, the speed will increase and vice versa. The level of automobilization has the opposite influence on speed of delivery. Urban delivery efficiency depends on a few factors, for example: speed of delivery, delivery quality, delivery time etc. Also, depends on this time, which may take place during peak and non-peak periods.

Traffic flow characteristics showed different behaviour in peak and off-peak (non-peak) periods. Each of these periods is observed during the day in any city. In the peak period there is a dense flow, and the movement of all vehicles in it slows down. The ability to manoeuvre there is limited. These conditions are usually observed in the morning and evening hours when everyone is going to their place of work, study, etc. The evening peak is less pronounced since the flows coming from the place of work and study, etc. can be distributed according to additional purposes of the tours (shops, cinemas, other activities).

In the non-peak period, a non-dense flow is characterized by the presence of vehicles on the road that does not interfere with manoeuvres on the road. This condition is observed when most drivers have already arrived at their main destination. The non-peak period is also can be characterized by single cars on the road. The driver can freely choose any permissible speed and save fuel at the same time [5]. Peak and non-peak periods affect the delivery time, distance, and speed of delivery.

Time limits of peak and off-peak may vary for different cities. This is due to the liveability of the rhythms of cities and the different urban traffic. The researchers considered that inhabitants have most movements in the morning and evening peak hours. During the non-peak period, the urban traffic is much less than during the peak, which leads to a reduction in delivery time and an increase the sustainability.

The aim of the paper is assessment of urban freight delivery during peak and off-peak traffic periods. The objectives of paper are:

- Form a method of assessment. Analyse and evaluate factors affecting speed of delivery,
- Determine the rate of delivery to different traffic density during the day (peak, non-peak),
- To estimate the impact of the capacity of the vehicle on the speed of delivery,
- Assess the urban delivery tours efficiency with different traffic periods.

3 Experimental Research

The survey is made through the polling of the transport industry. The Form has been used to implement the survey, see Fig. 1. The questionnaire is structured as follows. The first section contains the information of vehicle. It consists of different characteristics of freight vehicle. The second part connected to the operation of the driver and vehicle.

1. Vehicle information

1.1 Brand		1.2 Model		1.3 Capacity, t	
1.6 Plates				1.4 Capacity, m³	
1.7 Additional information				1.5 Type of loading and unloading	

2. Operation of the driver and vehicle

2.1 Operation	2.2 Indicating of Time starting operation, hh:mm	2.3 Speedometer Indicator, km	2.4 Actual Time of operation, min
Starting the garage			
Ending the Garage			

3. Operation tasks

3.1 №	3.2 Location, Address	3.3 Name of pick-up or delivery point	3.4 Indicating of Time operation (starts, ends), hh:mm- hh:mm	2.3 Speedometer Indicator, km	3.5 Type of operation	3.6 Type of goods	3.7 Amount of goods, ton	3.8 Number of pallets (boxes), units	3.9 Notes about loading and unloading technology
1									
2									

Fig. 1. Form for record keeper

The last part connected to the routes stops on the routes where the fixation of time, and distance were made. The section "Operation tasks" has current information about all parts of the route. The record keeper paid attention for each activity. For example, changing location or vehicle utilisation rate. This person has been fixating these indicators during the delivery process.

According to the survey 36 records were explored for transportation service of different retail networks. At the set result was considered: quantity of stops on route, volume (amount) of distribution, the total distance by route, time window in which the selection was conducted, the capacity of vehicle etc. The time window of day is used to detect the "peak hour" and "non-peak hour" of the movement of vehicles and to determine its impact on the speed, which is shown in table 1. Different vehicles were used for the same freight network to establish the influence of vehicle capacity on the speed of delivery.

An experiment was carried out to conduct the research. Routes were built with different vehicles (capacity 3–10 tons, brand, from euro-3 to euro-6, type of fuel) for the retail networks. The one route was chosen with the largest quantity of retailers. Thus, 12 routes were received. Further, the received data on the routes are entered into the program "Statgraphics" [25].

Table 1. Range of data variation for speed model.

q_n, t^a	T, min[b]	L, km[c]	V_t, km/h[d]	T, min	L, km	V_t, km/h
	peak period			non-peak period		
3	1,23	18,081	14,66	1,57	18,081	21,5
3	1,57	18,081	11,54	3,38	22,138	15,55
5	1,63	22,138	13,55	3,38	28,239	8,35
5	3,63	22,138	6,09	1,82	28,398	21,6
7,5	2,15	28,239	13,13	0,98	25,166	35,68
7,5	3,9	28,239	16,24	1,1	25,617	28,29
10	1,48	28,398	15,14	1,38	33,388	24,19
10	2,28	28,398	12,44	1,5	33,839	22,56
3	1	25,166	25,17	1,65	13,091	17,93
3	0,98	25,166	25,59	1,5	32,002	31,33
5	1,1	25,617	23,29	3	43,666	14,56
5	1,1	25,617	23,29	3,25	48,681	19,98
7,5	1,57	33,388	21,31	1,57	18,081	21,52
7,5	1,43	33,388	18,29	1,47	22,138	25,06
10	1,68	33,839	10,1	2,85	28,239	15,91
10	2,5	33,839	13,54	1,7	28,398	22,7
3	0,83	13,091	15,71	0,93	21,423	33,04
3	1,6	13,091	18,18	1,13	24,2	31,42
5	1,9	32,002	16,84	1,18	25,048	31,23
5	1,5	32,002	21,33	1,68	25,048	19,91
7,5	2,2	43,666	14,85	1,08	14,622	23,54
7,5	3,62	43,666	12,07	1,55	34,17	32,05
10	2,48	48,681	9,6	1,38	34,17	34,76
10	3,97	48,681	12,27	1,38	34,17	34,6
3	1,57	18,081	21,54	1,57	18,081	21,52
5	2,32	22,138	19,56	1,48	22,138	24,96
7,5	3,88	28,239	14,27	3,1	28,239	13,11
10	1,88	28,398	15,08	1,87	28,398	20,19
3	0,93	21,423	22,95	0,93	21,423	33,04
5	1,13	24,2	21,35	0,95	24,2	35,47
7,5	1,22	25,048	20,59	1,23	25,048	30,36

(*continued*)

Table 1. (*continued*)

q_n, t[a]	T, min[b]	L, km[c]	V_t, km/h[d]	T, min	L, km	V_t, km/h
10	1,35	25,048	18,55	2,02	25,048	17,4
3	1,17	14,622	22,53	1,25	14,622	21,7
5	1,55	34,17	22,05	1,88	34,17	28,18
7,5	1,72	34,17	15,9	1,55	34,17	32,05
10	1,55	34,17	12,05	2,55	34,17	16,4

[a]Capacity of vehicle
[b]Delivery time
[c]Length of route
[d]Route speed

4 Results

Regression and correlation analysis were used in processing the obtained data. The following equations are then obtained using the software "Statgraphics" for the peak
hour:

$$V_t = 45,405 \cdot \beta - 1,52513 \cdot N_p - 0,945548 \cdot q_n, \tag{1}$$

where V_t – average speed of delivery, km/h; β – the empty running rate factor. The rate
of empty running vehicles is the rate of vehicle-kilometres without goods or passengers;
N_p – quantity of retailers, un.; q_n – capacity of vehicle, t.

And for non-peak hour the researchers also used the "Statgraphics":

$$Vt = 0,395976 \cdot L + 16,5456 \cdot \gamma, \tag{2}$$

where L – the length of the route, km; γ – load utilisation factor.

The parameters of statistical assess of models showed in Table 2 and the confidence
intervals present in Table 3.

Models are obtained using regression and correlation analyses. On the basis of these,
it is possible to construct graphs of dependence of the speed value on different coefficients. In a peak hour and a non-peak hour these indicators differ. The results indicate
that in different time periods the speed of the vehicle is influenced by different indicators
(Fig. 2 and 3).

The speed per peak hour is influenced by the empty running rate for road transport
(Fig. 1, a), capacity of vehicle (Fig. 2, b) and quantity of retailers (Fig. 2, c).

Figure 1(a) shows the empty running rate for road transport in this research changed
from 0,56 to 0,95. On the graph, see when this parameter decreases, the speed increases.
If you consider that the rate of empty running vehicles is the rate of vehicle-kilometres
without goods, then without goods, a freight vehicle moves more easily on the road.
According to Fig. 2(b), when the capacity of a vehicle increases, the speed will decrease
and vice versa. This dependence can be explained by the fact that a vehicle with a lower
capacity is easier to manage and manoeuvre along urban streets. The number of retailers

Table 2. Statistical assess of models.

Indicator	Traffic period during the day	
	non-peak hour	peak hour
T-Statistic: Tabular coefficient	1,97	1,97
The empty running rate for road transport	–	11,4564
Capacity of vehicle	–	−3,04769
Quantity of retailers	–	−5,13999
The length of the route	3,59496	–
Load capacity utilization function	4,46854	–
F-Ratio: Tabular coefficient	161	161
Calculated	168,14	184,59
R-squared	90,8178	94,3759
R-squared (adjusted for d.f.)	90,5477	94,035
Mean absolute error	6,21639	3,54909

Table 3. 95% confidence interval for the coefficient in the model.

Coefficient in the model	Lower limit	Upper limit
Peak hour		
The empty running rate for road transport, β	37,3416	53,4683
Quantity of retailers, Np	−2,12881	−0,92145
Capacity of vehicle, q_n	−1,57676	−0,31434
Non-peak hour		
The length of the route	3,59496	–
Load utilization factor	4,46854	–

(Fig. 2, c) had decreased and increased during the speed increase. The greater the number of retailers, the greater the area of the urban area covered by the route. It passes through more intersections and turns than a vehicle with fewer retailers.

The speed of delivery per non-peak hour is influenced by the length of route (Fig. 3, a) and load capacity utilisation function (Fig. 3, b).

Figure 2(a) had the next dependence: when the length of the route increased, the speed of delivery also increased. With an increase in the length of the route, the manoeuvrability of the vehicle increases, space for acceleration, and braking at the end of the path when approaching the last retailer. The load utilization factor function (Fig. 2, b) has an influence on speed of delivery, such as the previous parameter.

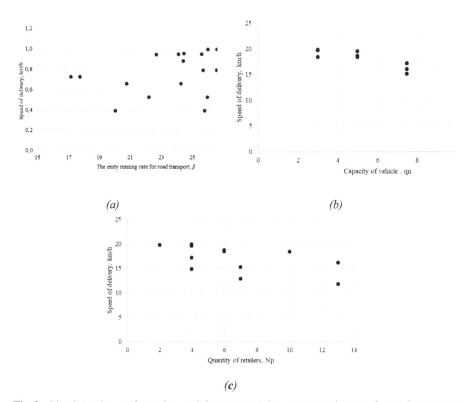

Fig. 2. The dependence of speed at peak hour on: *(a)* the empty running rate for road transport; *(b)* capacity of vehicle; *(c)* quantity of retailers.

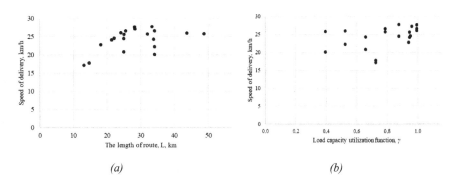

Fig. 3. Dependence of speed of delivery at peak hour on: *(a)* a length of route; *(b)* load capacity utilization function.

5 Assessment of the Efficiency of Urban Delivery Tours with Peak and Off-Peak Periods

Based on the data obtained, the value of speeds of delivery in different periods for vehicles with different carrying capacities was selected in the work. The corresponding graph is plotted in Fig. 4. It is clearly visible how the speed changes depending on the period per day under investigation. On the basis of a significant change in the speed parameter, the urban delivery tours also change. When the speed of delivery values are the highest during the non-peak period, the vehicle's delivery time will be the lowest.

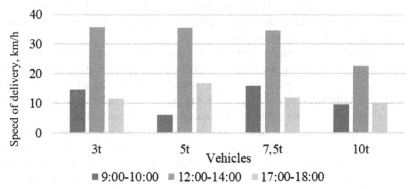

Fig. 4. The dependence of the speed of delivery on peak (9:00–10:00, 17:00–18:00) and non-peak (12:00–14:00) periods.

Therefore, the speed of delivery of the vehicle directly affects the delivery time. The average time on the route will be longer for delivery during the peak period. It should also be noted that there may come a time when it becomes unprofitable to serve the retail network without considering time periods. After all, a vehicle leaving during the peak (9:00–10:00) hour can deliver a container load during the non-peak period. When, considering the time periods, these goods will arrive at the same time, but without losing time on the road during peak hours.

6 Conclusion

This research makes it possible to use an existing improved approach to determining the speed of delivery in the logistics system. When estimating regression models, parameters such as speed of delivery, capacity of the vehicles, length of route, delivery time, etc. The model of change of time of day of transportation for peak hour and non-peak hour is constructed. With the help of the field survey, data was obtained based on retail network routes for research. Also, an experiment, which is the basis for building models. The resulting models allow one to calculate the speed of delivery of goods by vehicles. In a logistics system, it can be used to manage the delivery of goods in real time. This will allow for a more accurately determine the parameters of retail networks and predict the state of the logistics system.

The speed of delivery is one of the speeds that are calculated during operational planning. Although this speed is the main one in the operational planning of transport processes, using this approach can be used for tactical or strategic planning (for example: expanding or changing the number of retailers and determining the predicted parameters of transport operation in this case).

The method of obtaining data to build models was the use of the recording parameters in road. This research is limited by the following parameters: the example was calculated for one city, in a certain period of the year (velocity data may differ in winter and summer). Although the calculations were carried out on the example of one city, the results may be valid for other similar cities (similar in urban planning, area, etc.). The efficiency depends on the choice of travel periods. Since it depends on the delivery time, which can take place during peak and non-peak periods. The speed of delivery and time are very different in periods during the day.

Based on the vehicle results obtained, the speed of delivery depends on different parameters in different time periods. In the peak hour, the speed is affected by the empty running rate for road transport, capacity of vehicle and quantity of retailers, and the non-peak hour influenced by the length of route and load capacity utilisation function.

The analysis of scientific publications showed a different level of processing of material related to the development of freight transport under the conditions of sustainable development of cities by scientists from foreign countries and Ukrainian scientists. In our country, this direction of research is new and requires significant attention from both scientists and government officials. Conduct in-depth scientific research in the field of freight transportation under the conditions of sustainable urban development. When planning the operation of the urban freight transportation, it is necessary to consider the peculiarities of its implementation. This approach will allow local authorities to make informed decisions when planning urban spatial development and will also help to determine the list of basic requirements for entities that provide freight transportation, with the aim of optimising urban traffic. The planning of freight transport operations should be carried out consistently and thoroughly, covering all its elements and connections. An in-depth study of the demand and supply for the transportation of goods in the city will make it possible to form an effective strategy for the development of freight transport in the city. The analytical description and quantitative evaluation of the obtained results will create a basis for the development of a qualitative list of measures, the implementation of which will allow increasing the efficiency of urban freight transportation. The key aspects of the successful implementation of measures to improve the operation of freight transport are the financial support of the planned actions, their support by local self-government bodies, as well as the optimal organisation and coordination of the processes and actions of all planning participants. The implementation of such an interconnected set of actions will ensure the success of planning and implementation activities at all stages of its implementation.

References

1. Hriekova, O.: Analysis of urban freight distribution management methods on the principles of "Green Logistics". In: Smart Technologies in Urban Engineering: Proceedings of STUE-2022, pp. 820–830. Springer, Cham (2022). https://doi.org/10.1007/978-3-031-20141-7_73
2. Prasolenko, O., Burko, D., Tolmachov, I., Gyulyev, N., Galkin, A., Lobashov, O.: Creating safer routing for urban freight transportation. Transport. Res. Procedia **39**, 417–427 (2019)
3. Planning and design for sustainable urban mobility: global report on human settlements, vol. 317. United Nations Human Settlements Programme, New York (2013)
4. Nuzzolo, A., Crisalli, U., Comi, A.: A system of models for the simulation of urban freight restocking tours. Procedia Soc. Behav. Sci. **39**, 664–676 (2012)
5. Arvianto, A., Sopha, B.M., Asih, A.M.S., Imron, M.A.: City logistics challenges and innovative solutions in developed and developing economies: a systematic literature review. Int. J. Eng. Bus. Manag. **13** (2021)
6. Akyol, D.E., De Koster, R.B.: Determining time windows in urban freight transport: a city cooperative approach. Transport. Res. Part E: Logist. Transport. Rev. **118**, 34–50 (2018)
7. Liu, C., et al.: Time-dependent vehicle routing problem with time windows of city logistics with a congestion avoidance approach. Knowl.-Based Syst. **188**, 104813 (2020)
8. Cattaruzza, D., Absi, N., Feillet, D., González-Feliu, J.: Vehicle routing problems for city logistics. EURO J. Transport. Logist. **6**(1), 51–79 (2017)
9. Taniguchi, E., Thompson, R.G., Yamada, T.: Urban freight transporta-tion systems: a review of research, practice, and future challenges. Transp. Rev. **37**(3), 334–357 (2017)
10. Berman, B., Evans, J.: Urban goods movement: Balancing economic vitality and environmental sustainability. J. Transp. Geogr. **80**, 102469 (2019)
11. Holguín-Veras, J., Thorson, E., O'Brien, T., Cetin, M.: The impact of urban goods delivery restrictions on logistics operations: a review and a model for assessment. Transp. Rev. **37**(3), 308–333 (2017)
12. Cidell, J., Regan, A.: Urban freight and sustainability: a review of the literature and future research directions. Sustainability **10**(7), 2223 (2018)
13. Gerlough, D.L., Huber, M.J.: Measurement of flow, speed and concentration. In: Orland, H.P. (ed.) Traffic flow theory, 1st edn, no. 165, pp. 7–15. Transportation Research Board, Washington (1976)
14. Elvik, R.: Optimal speed limits: limits of optimality models. Transport. Res. Rec. **1818**(1), 32–38 (2002)
15. Davidich, N., Melenchuk, T., Kush, Y., Davidich, Y., Lobashov, O., Galkin, A.: Modelling truck's transportation speed on the route considering driver's state. Transport. Res. Procedia **30**, 207–215 (2018)
16. Huang, Y.-S., Weng, Y.-S., Weimin, W., Chen, B.-Y.: Control strategies for solving the problem of traffic congestion. IET Intel. Transp. Syst. **10**(10), 642–648 (2016)
17. Shepelev, V., Glushkov, A., Fadina, O., Gritsenko, A.: Comparative evaluation of road vehicle emissions at urban intersections with detailed traffic dynamics. Mathematics **10**(11), 1887 (2022). https://doi.org/10.3390/math10111887
18. Makarova, I.V., Belyaev, E.I., Mavrin, V.G., Suleimanov, I.F.: City transport system improvement through the use of simulation modeling system. Int. J. Appl. Eng. Res. **9**(22), 15649–15655 (2014)
19. Davidich, N., Galkin, A., Iwan, S., Kijewska, K., Chumachenko, I., Davidich, Y.: Monitoring of urban freight flows distribution considering the human factor. Sustain. Cities Soc. **75**, 103168 (2021)
20. Janic, M.: Modelling the full costs of an intermodal and road freight transport network. Transp. Res. Part D: Transp. Environ. **12**(1), 33–44 (2007)

21. Kijewska, K., Iwan, S.: Utilization of portable traffic detectors as the support for the data collection process in city logistics systems. Arch. Transp. Syst. Telematics **12**(1), 29–35 (2019)
22. Iwan, S., Małecki, K., Stalmach, D.: Utilization of mobile applications for the improvement of traffic management systems. In: Mikulski, J. (ed.) TST 2014. CCIS, vol. 471, pp. 48–58. Springer, Heidelberg (2014). https://doi.org/10.1007/978-3-662-45317-9_6
23. Galkin, A., Davidich, N., Filina-Dawidowicz, L., Davidich, Y.: Improving the safety of urban freight deliveries by organization of the transportation process considering driver's state. Transport. Res. Procedia **39**, 54–63 (2019)
24. Van Duin, J.H.R., de Goffau, W., Wiegmans, B., Tavasszy, L.A., Saes, M.: Improving home delivery efficiency by using principles of address intelligence for B2C deliveries. Transport. Res. Procedia **12**, 14–25 (2016)
25. Kush, Y., Skrypin, V., Galkin, A., Dolia, K., Tkachenko, I., Davidich, N.: Regularities of change of the supply chain operation efficiency, depending on the parameters of the transport process. Transport. Res. Procedia **30**, 216–225 (2018)

Workshop: Towards Open Data Practices at the International Conference on the Internet of Everything

Natalie Kiesler[(✉)]

DIPF Leibniz Institute for Research and Information in Education,
Frankfurt am Main, Germany
kiesler@dipf.de

Abstract. The Internet of Everything (IoE) has the potential to transform the way we live, work, and interact with the world around us. It involves the connection of billions of devices and sensors, generating vast amounts of data that can be used to inform decision-making, improve efficiency, and drive innovation. However, realizing the full potential of the IoE requires the adoption of open data practices, which can increase transparency, provenance, and accountability. This workshop aims to discuss pathways toward open data practices in the context of the IoE by bringing together practitioners in the field. The workshop will include intensive discussions with participants about their experiences with the publication of research data (including software) in the IoE context, but also challenges, concerns, and barriers to publishing research data. The workshop further addresses possible publication formats, how and where to publish data, questions of data ownership, as well as common formats and types. By discussing the state-of-the-art within the IoE community, we intend to draw conclusions on a path forward towards open data practices at venues, such as the IoE Con, as these practices have implications for future conference submissions, tracks, and review processes. Finally, by promoting open data practices, we can unleash the full potential of the IoE to create a more connected, smarter, and sustainable future.

Keywords: Internet of Everything · Open Data · Open Science · FAIR principles

1 Introduction

The Internet of Everything (IoE) can be defined as *"a distributed network of connections between people, smart things, processes, and data, whereas these components interact and exchange real-time data"* [13]. The connections between these four pillars comprise people-to-people (P2P), machine-to-machine (M2M), and people-to-machine (P2M) systems. Hence, technologies within the IoE context

© ICST Institute for Computer Sciences, Social Informatics and Telecommunications Engineering 2024
Published by Springer Nature Switzerland AG 2024. All Rights Reserved
T. Pereira et al. (Eds.): IOECON 2023, LNICST 551, pp. 139–143, 2024.
https://doi.org/10.1007/978-3-031-51572-9_11

are data-intensive with respect to the exchange of information, and the development of new technologies, interfaces, and systems, as they constantly produce research data, including software.

Unfortunately, publishing research data is still a challenge in many scientific disciplines [3]. Especially the submission of research data including software is currently subject to discussions within several areas of computing [2,8–10]. Among the challenges are the lack of recognition [15], and the lack of FAIRness [1,6,16,19] for primary researchers who need to invest great efforts to produce mature data. At the same time, the majority of published research data (including software) is based on natural language reports limited in length, automatically lacking depth and detail, and adding ambiguity. Further demands towards publishing research data may comprise high (code) quality, documentation [11,14], or method reports [12] – all of which take time to produce. By the time a researcher reaches the desired maturity, deadlines may have passed, or technologies may be outdated. Moreover, guidelines or procedures for the peer review of software, huge data sets, and/or other technologies have not yet been established. After all, the benefits of publishing such research artifacts remain low. The same is true for the context of the Internet of Everything (IoE) as an emerging field.

The other extreme may be that research data are not even required for a conference publication or journal and that the peer review of submitted data is purely optional [16]. Instructions for authors and reviewers often state: "Reviewers are not required to review your supplementary materials, your paper submission must stand on its own" [4], or "Papers are expected to stand alone, and not to require the reading of supplementary information" [7]. These instructions can be considered a stimulus for authors not to submit their research data at all, not even for the camera-ready version. Eventually, it can lead to less transparent and less comprehensive research studies and publications, which are challenging to reproduce or replicate.

With the International Conference on the Internet of Everything (IoE Con), a new conference is being established that will help shape the direction of this area, and how the community will handle respective research data including software and IT infrastructure. It is, therefore, crucial to start developing guidelines and procedures for (1) the submission of research data to conferences like the IoE Con, (2) the review of research data by peers, and (3) the publication of research data within certain conference tracks and proceedings, or perhaps even alternative formats. Designing a path towards open data practices now will thus strengthen and improve research in the IoE field and the computing community in the long run.

2   Goals of the Workshop

As software and research data are not a byproduct of the epistemological process, it only appears natural to make data available to other researchers, e.g., by applying the FAIR principles [19] and making data findable, accessible, interoperable, and reusable. At the same time, open data strategies and guidelines have been promoted for years in the U.S. and in Europe [5,17,18]. However, it is still challenging to transfer these principles to software and technology [8,9], which is why we need to involve the research community and consider their challenges and barriers.

As one of the first steps on a pathway towards open data practices at IoE Con, the facilitator of this workshop intends to address the following objectives:

1. Increase the community's consciousness of the role and impact of open data practices.
2. Gather the community perspective with regard to challenges, barriers, and possible strategies to overcome them.
3. Develop realistic, and comprehensible requirements for the publication of research data (including software) at IoE Con.
4. Start designing peer review guidelines for the IoE Con program committee.
5. Discuss new publication formats or tracks in the context of the IoE Con.

The expected result of the workshop is the exploration of realistic publication formats and peer review procedures for the IoE community. Gathering this perspective will help inform the IoECon program committee on how to realize open data practices in the near future.

3 Workshop Schedule

The workshop is intended to last three hours and address the aforementioned goals by discussing and elaborating on them with the workshop's participants. The activities will be arranged as follows:

- Provide an initial input from the literature about the well-known challenges and barriers for researchers (15 min)
- Give insights into existing review processes from other conferences (15 min)
- Discuss the community's prior experience with regard to the publication of research data (including software) based on a set of guiding questions (45 min)
- Short break (15 min)
- Use expert groups (or alternatively breakout sessions) to discuss the following three guiding questions (30 min):
  - What are realistic, comprehensive requirements for the publication of research data at IoECon?
  - What are feasible peer review guidelines that can serve as recommendations for the IoECon program committee?
  - Consider new publication formats or tracks for IoECon.
- Presentation and discussion of each group's input and ideas to derive concrete recommendations and a path for action (45 min, with 3 groups à 15 min)
- Summary of the main takeaways and wrap-up of the workshop (15 min)

The workshop may be realized online or in presence, although participation may be higher in an online format. In that case, discussions and group work will be realized via Zoom breakout rooms.

4   Expected Results and Publication

This new workshop format serves as a networking opportunity within the IoE community, as it allows researchers to connect and exchange their ideas and concerns related to open data and open science practices.

Moreover, all groups will be asked to document their discussions in shared documents (e.g., on a flipchart or in an online file). Moreover, the facilitator of the workshop will track the community's input during the entire workshop, especially as part of the presentation and discussion of the subgroups' results, and as part of the summary of take-aways.

This workshop will further serve as a basis for a submission to next year's IoE Con, as the facilitator will compile the community's ideas and course for action into a workshop report. Upon positive review by the program committee, it will be included in the 2024 conference proceedings.

5   Conclusion

The proposed workshop on open data practices at the International Conference on the Internet of Everything aims to address the challenges and barriers of publishing research data including software from the perspective of IoE researchers and practitioners. The IoE is a data-intensive field that develops new technologies and produces huge amounts of research data. We, therefore, need to start developing a path forward to mitigate the well-known challenges of data publications due to the lack of recognition and FAIRness. The workshop's goals are to increase the community's consciousness of open data practices, gather the community's experience with publishing research data, develop realistic and comprehensible requirements for software publication, start designing peer review guidelines, and discuss new publication formats. The expected result is the exploration of realistic publication formats and recommendations for peer review procedures for the IoE community, helping inform the IoECon program committee on how to realize open data practices in the near future. To conclude, the proposed workshop is an essential step toward open data practices, and it will strengthen and improve research in the IoE field.

References

1. Barker, M., et al.: Introducing the fair principles for research software. Sci. Data **9**(1), 622 (2022). https://doi.org/10.1038/s41597-022-01710-x
2. Beardsley, M., Hernández-Leo, D., Ramirez-Melendez, R.: Seeking reproducibility: assessing a multimodal study of the testing effect. J. Comput. Assist. Learn. **34**(4), 378–386 (2018). https://doi.org/10.1111/jcal.12265
3. Borgman, C.L., Pasquetto, I.V.: Why data sharing and reuse are hard to do (2017). https://escholarship.org/uc/item/0jj17309
4. CHI: Papera - Quick Facts (2022). https://chi2022.acm.org/for-authors/presenting/papers/

5. European Union: European open science cloud (2023). https://eosc-portal.eu/
6. Hong, N.P.C., et al.: Fair principles for research software (FAIR4RS principles) (2022). https://doi.org/10.15497/RDA00065
7. ITiCSE: Call for papers (2023). https://iticse.acm.org/2023/call-for-papers/
8. Jay, C., Haines, R., Katz, D.S.: Software must be recognised as an important output of scholarly research. arXiv preprint arXiv:2011.07571 (2020)
9. Katz, D.S., Gruenpeter, M., Honeyman, T.: Taking a fresh look at fair for research software. Patterns **2**(3), 100222 (2021). https://doi.org/10.1016/j.patter.2021.100222
10. Katz, D.S., Psomopoulos, F.E., Castro, L.J.: Working towards understanding the role of FAIR for machine learning. In: DaMaLOS, pp. 1–6 (2021). https://www.danielskatz.org/papers/FAIR4ML_for_DAMALOS.pdf
11. Kiesler, N.: Dataset: recursive problem solving in the online learning environment codingbat by computer science students (2022). https://doi.org/10.21249/DZHW:studentsteps:1.0.0
12. Kiesler, N.: Daten- und Methodenbericht Rekursive Problemlösung in der Online Lernumgebung CodingBat durch Informatik-Studierende. Technical report (2022). https://metadata.fdz.dzhw.eu/public/files/data-packages/stu-studentsteps$/attachments/studentsteps_Data_Methods_Report_de.pdf
13. Kiesler, N., Impagliazzo, J.: Perspectives on the internet of everything. In: Pereira, T., Impagliazzo, J., Santos, H. (eds.) IoECon 2022. LNICST, vol. 458, pp. 3–17. Springer, Cham (2023). https://doi.org/10.1007/978-3-031-25222-8_1
14. Kiesler, N., Pfülb, B.: Higher education programming competencies: a novel dataset. In: Iliadis, L., Papaleonidas, A., Angelov, P., Jayne, C. (eds) ICANN 2023. LNCS, vol. 14261, pp. 319–330. Springer, Cham (2023). https://doi.org/10.1007/978-3-031-44198-1_27, https://github.com/nkiesler-cs/HEPComp-Dataset
15. Kiesler, N., Schiffner, D.: On the lack of recognition of software artifacts and IT infrastructure in educational technology research. In: Henning, P.A., Striewe, M., Wölfel, M. (eds.) 20. Fachtagung Bildungstechnologien (DELFI), pp. 201–206. Gesellschaft für Informatik e.V., Bonn (2022). https://doi.org/10.18420/delfi2022-034
16. Kiesler, N., Schiffner, D.: Why we need open data in computer science education research. In: Proceedings of the 2023 Conference on Innovation and Technology in Computer Science Education, ITiCSE 2023, vol. 1. Association for Computing Machinery, New York (2023). https://doi.org/10.1145/3587102.3588860
17. National Science Foundation: Open data at NSF (2013). https://www.nsf.gov/data/
18. Pilat, D., Fukasaku, Y.: OECD principles and guidelines for access to research data from public funding. Data Sci. J. **6**, OD4–OD11 (2007). https://www.oecd.org/sti/inno/38500813.pdf
19. Wilkinson, M.D., et al.: The fair guiding principles for scientific data management and stewardship. Sci. Data **3**(1), 1–9 (2016). https://doi.org/10.1038/sdata.2016.18

Author Index

T. Pereira et al. (Eds.): IOECON 2023, LNICST 551, p. 145, 2024.
https://doi.org/10.1007/978-3-031-51572-9

Printed in the United States
by Baker & Taylor Publisher Services